BEST OF THE BIG BANDS

ISBN 0-634-03752-8

HAL•LEONARD®
CORPORATION

7777 W. Bluemound Rd. P.O. Box 13819 Milwaukee, WI 53213

Visit Hal Leonard Online at
www.halleonard.com

AQUELLOS OJOS VERDES
(Green Eyes)

Music by NILO MENENDEZ
Spanish Words by ADOLFO UTRERA
English Words by E. RIVERA and E. WOODS

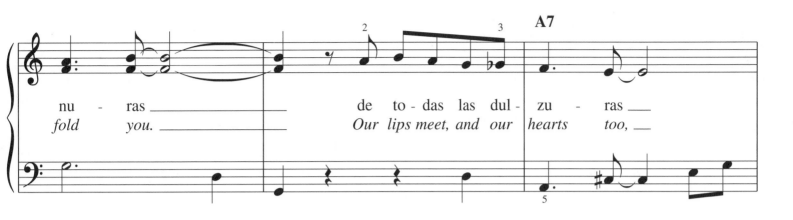

nu - ras _____ de to - das las dul - zu - ras _____
fold *you.* _____ *Our lips meet, and our hearts too,* _____

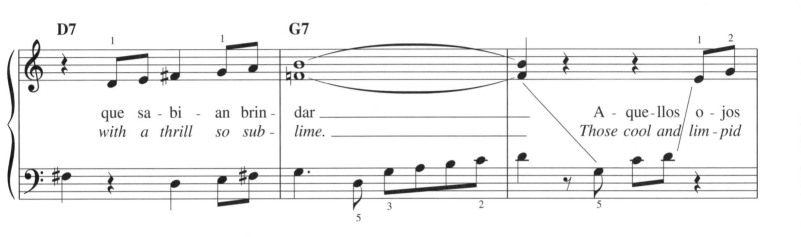

que sa - bi - an brin - dar _____ A - que - llos o - jos
with a thrill so sub - *lime.* _____ *Those cool and lim - pid*

ver - des _____ se - re - nos co - mo un la - go _____
green eyes, _____ *a pool where - in my love lies* _____

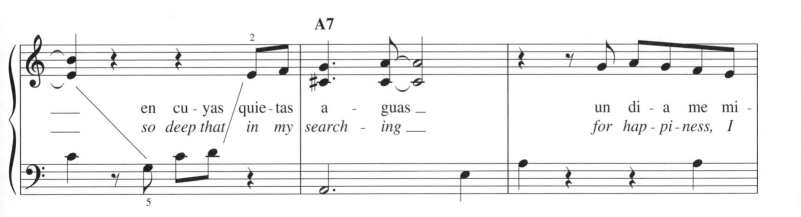

en cu - yas quie - tas a - guas _____ un di - a me mi -
so deep that in my search - ing _____ *for hap - pi - ness, I*

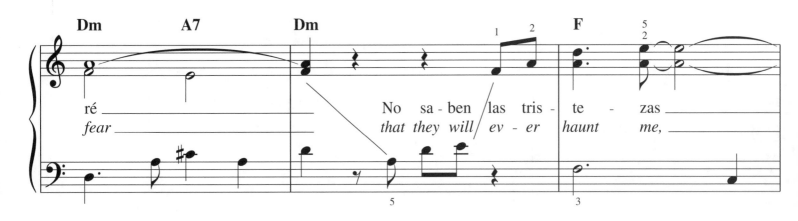

Dm   **A7**   **Dm**   **F**

ré _____ No sa - ben las tris - te - zas _____
fear _____ *that they will ev - er haunt me,* _____

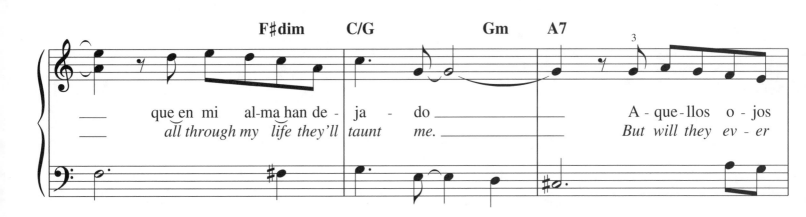

F♯dim   **C/G**   **Gm**   **A7**

___ que en mi al-ma han de - ja - do _____ A - que-llos o - jos
___ *all through my life they'll taunt me.* _____ *But will they ev - er*

D7   **G7**   **1.** **C**   **C♯dim**

ver - des ___ que yo nun - ca be - sa - ré.
want me? ___ *Green eyes, make my dreams come true.*

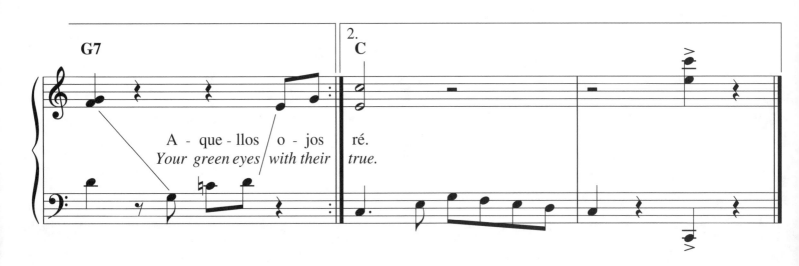

G7   **2.** **C**

A - que - llos o - jos ré.
Your green eyes with their true.

I'LL BE SEEING YOU
from RIGHT THIS WAY

Lyric by IRVING KAHAL
Music by SAMMY FAIN

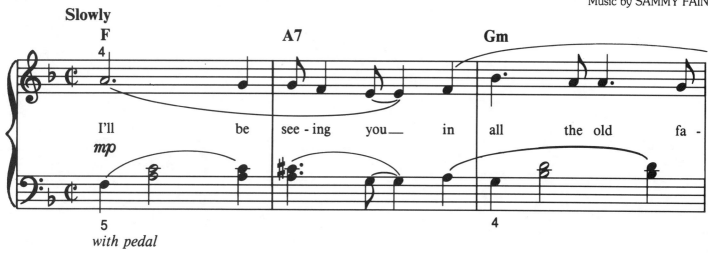

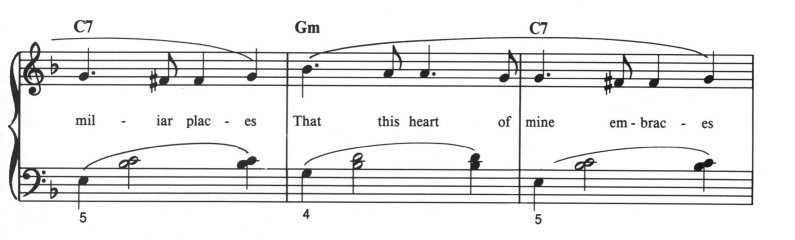

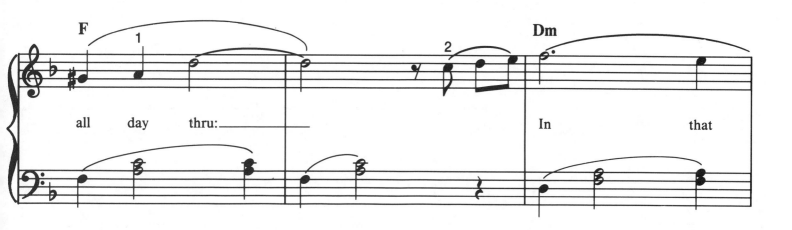

6

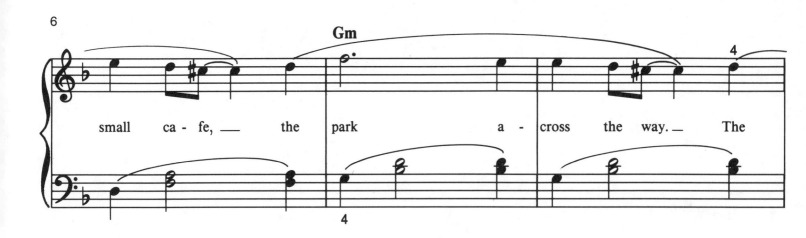

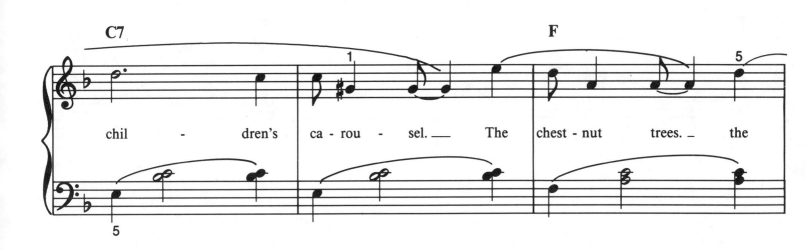

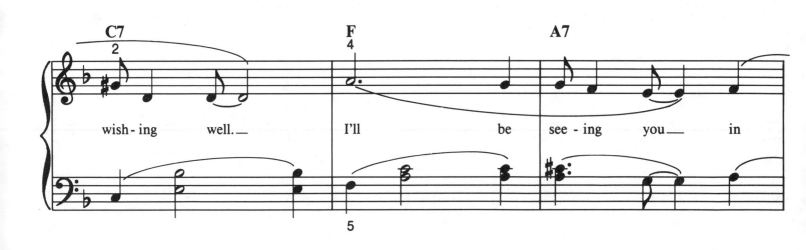

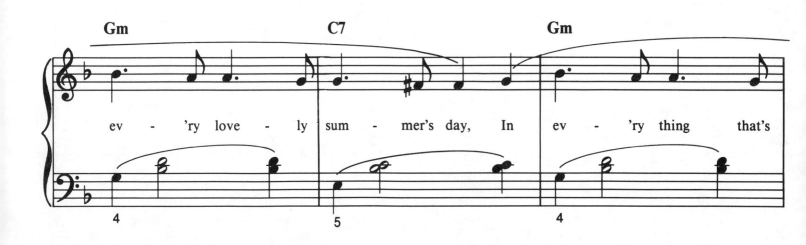

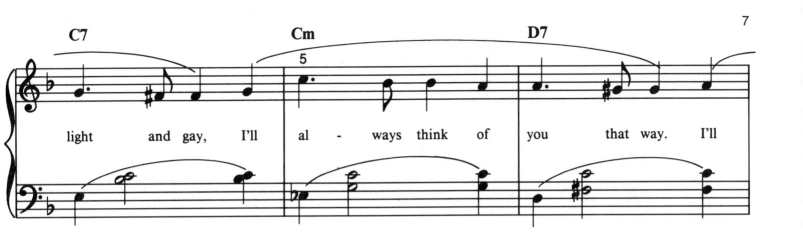

light and gay, I'll al - ways think of you that way. I'll

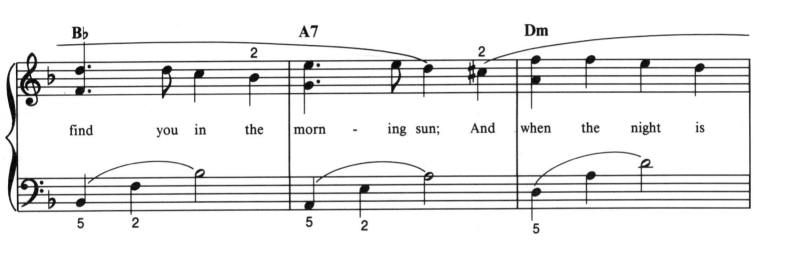

find you in the morn - ing sun; And when the night is

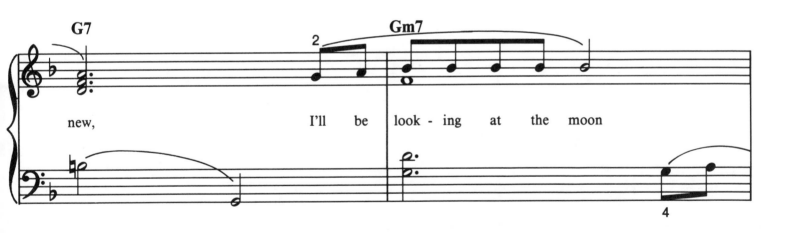

new, I'll be look - ing at the moon

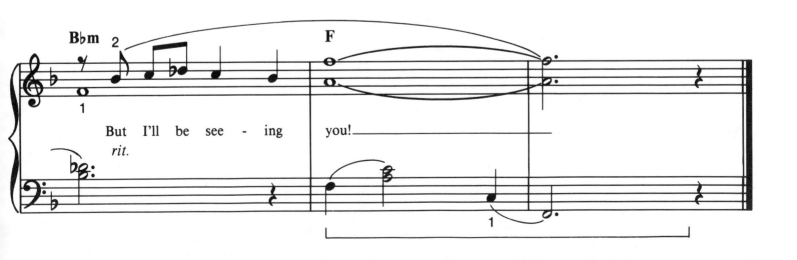

But I'll be see - ing you!

BÉSAME MUCHO
(Kiss Me Much)

Music and Spanish Words by CONSUELO VELAZQUEZ
English Words by SUNNY SKYLAR

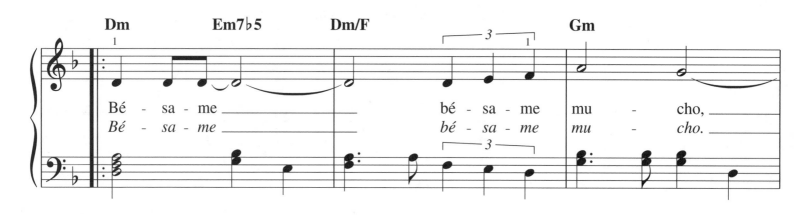

Bé - sa - me _____ bé - sa - me mu - cho, _____
Bé - sa - me _____ bé - sa - me mu - cho. _____

co - mo si fue - ra es - tá no - che la úl - ti - ma
Each time I cling to your kiss I hear mu - sic di -

vez; Bé -
vine. Bé -

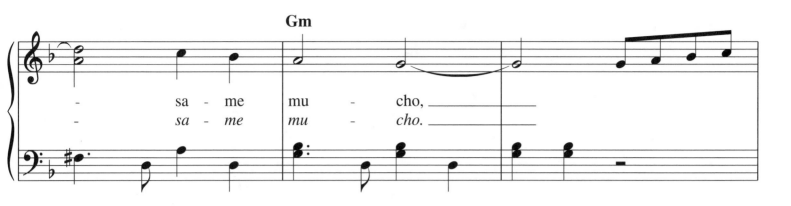

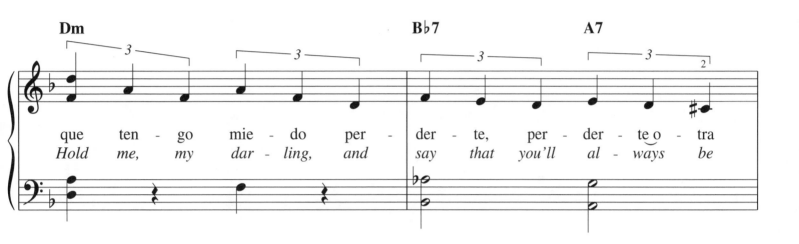

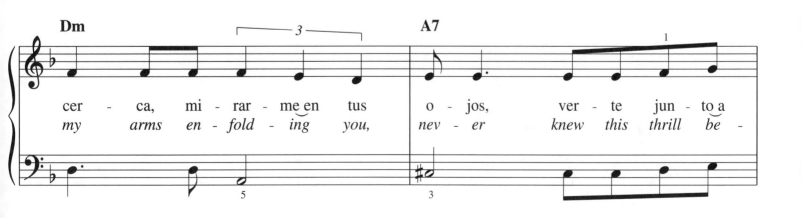

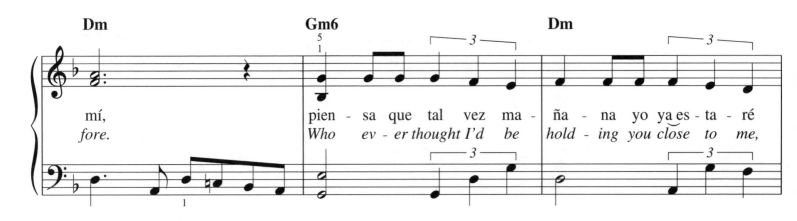

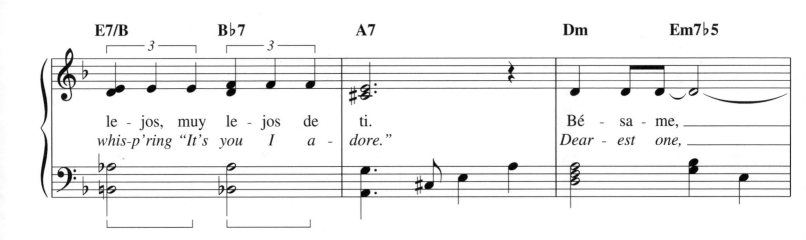

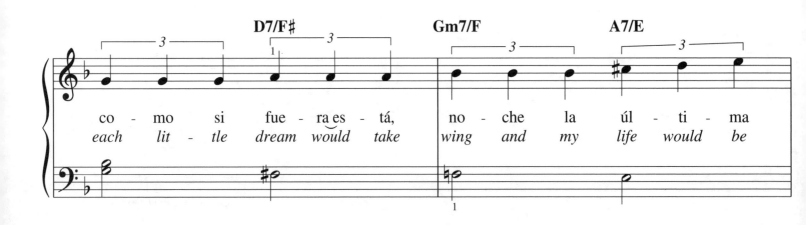

vez.
through.

Dm   **D7**   Bé -
     Bé -

Gm

- sa - me mu - cho. _____
- *sa - me mu - cho.* _____

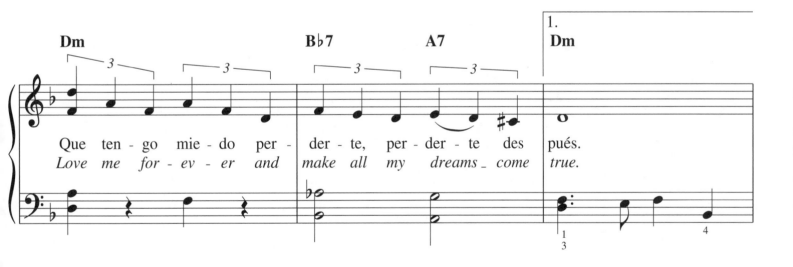

Dm   **B♭7**   **A7**   **1.** **Dm**

Que ten - go mie - do per - der - te, per - der - te des pués.
Love me for - ev - er and make all my dreams ＿ come true.

A7   **2.** **Dm**

pués.
true.

BODY AND SOUL

Words by EDWARD HEYMAN,
ROBERT SOUR and FRANK EYTON
Music by JOHN GREEN

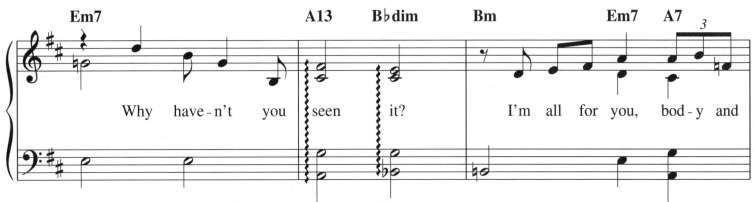

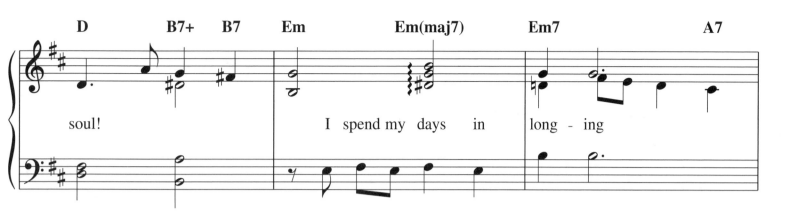

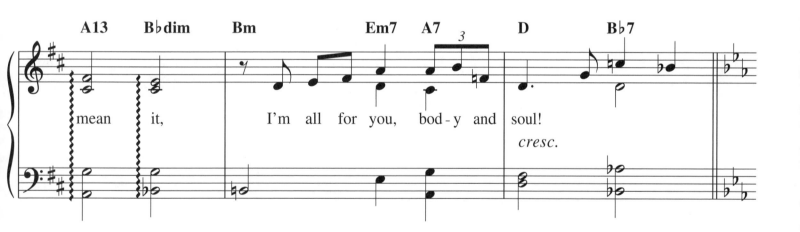

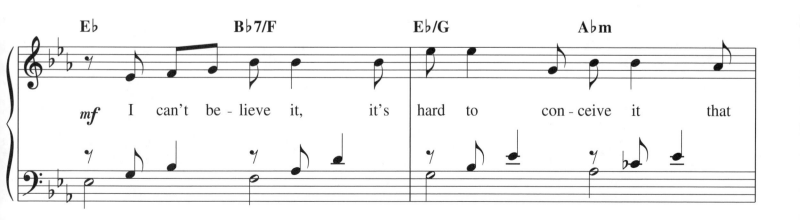

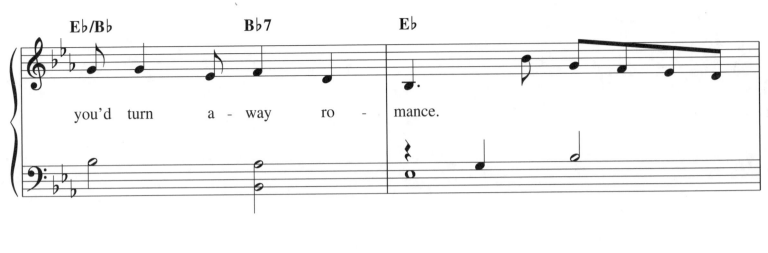

you'd turn a - way ro - mance.

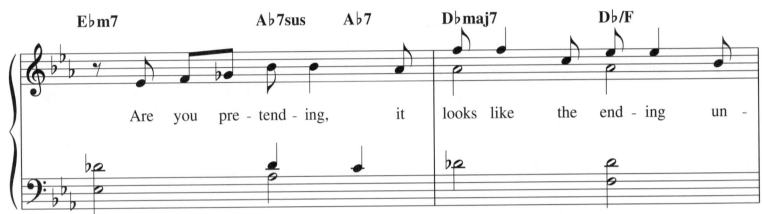

Are you pre - tend - ing, it looks like the end - ing un -

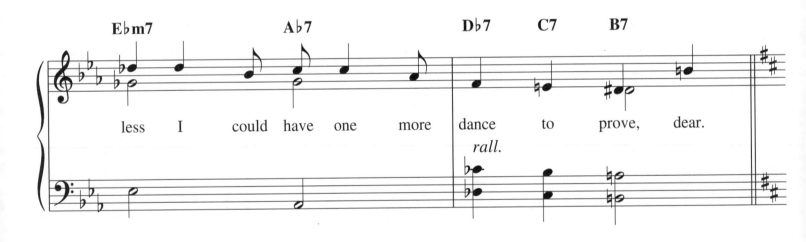

less I could have one more dance to prove, dear.

rall.

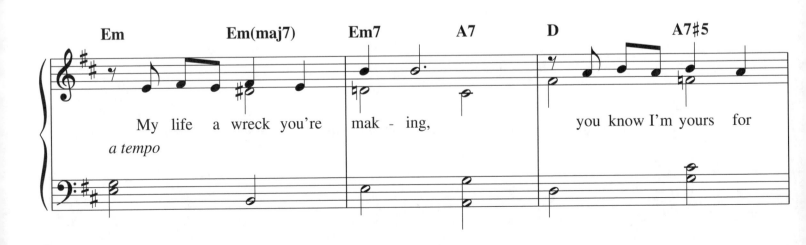

My life a wreck you're mak - ing, you know I'm yours for

a tempo

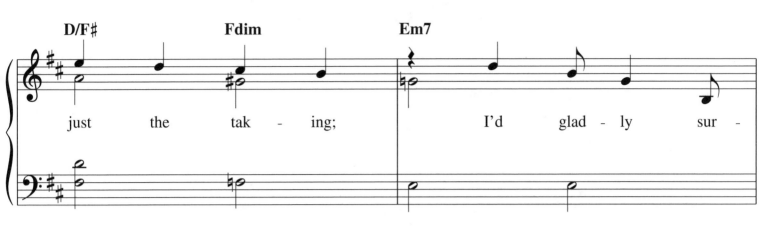

just the tak - ing; I'd glad - ly sur -

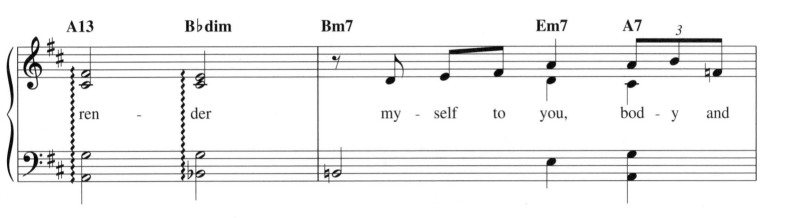

ren - der my - self to you, bod - y and

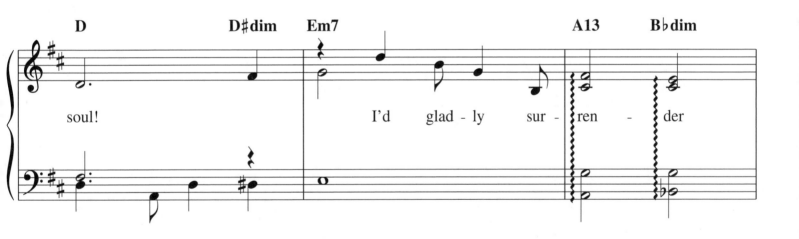

soul! I'd glad - ly sur - ren - der

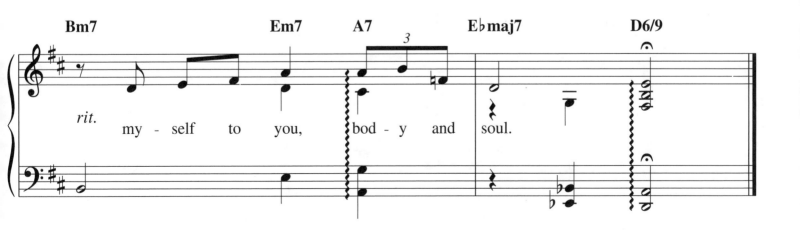

rit. my - self to you, bod - y and soul.

CHEROKEE
(Indian Love Song)

Words and Music by
RAY NOBLE

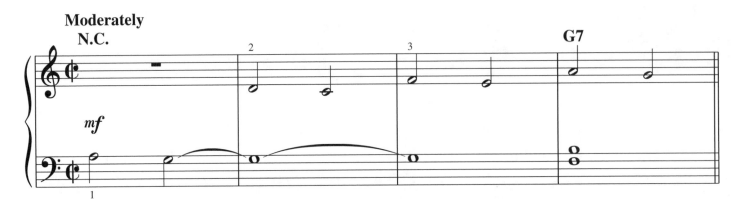

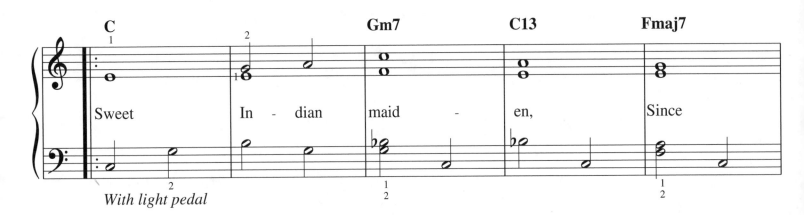

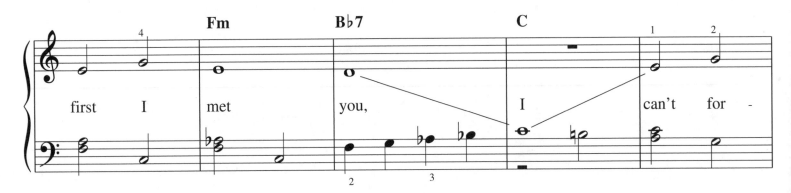

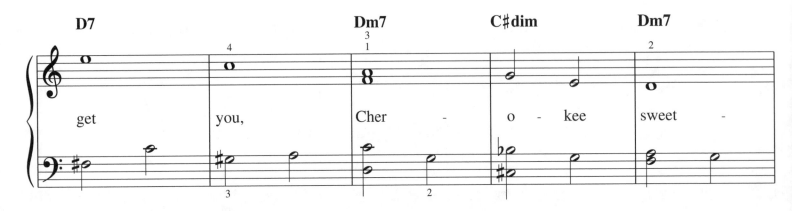

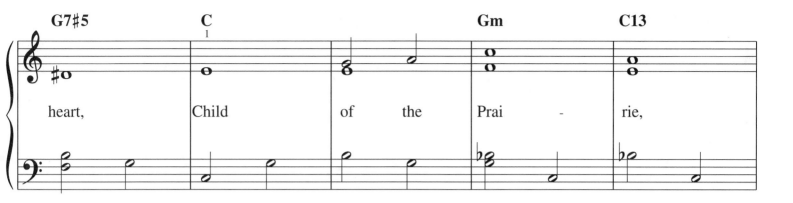

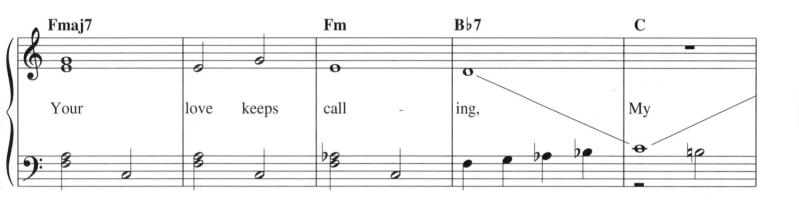

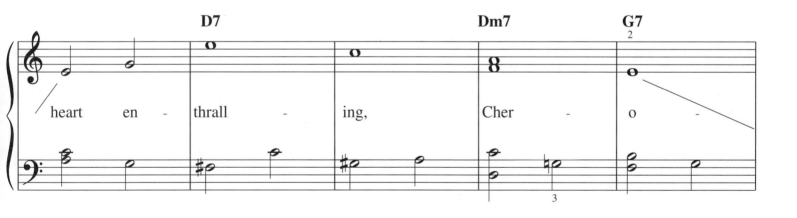

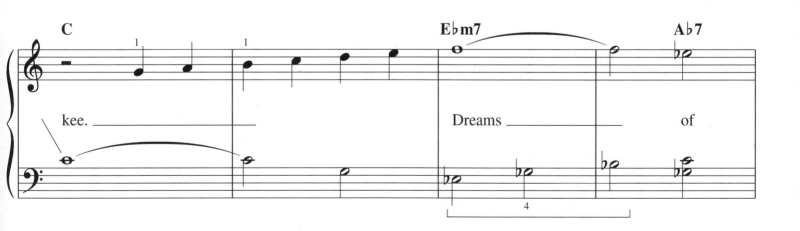

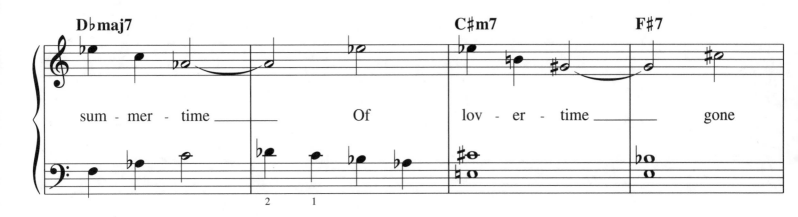

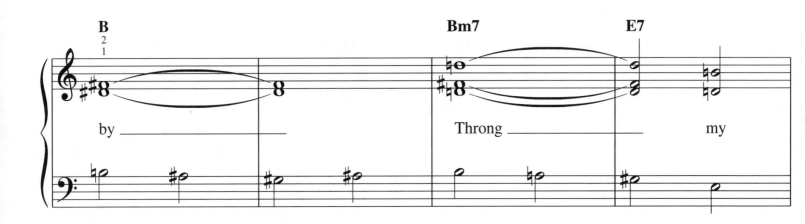

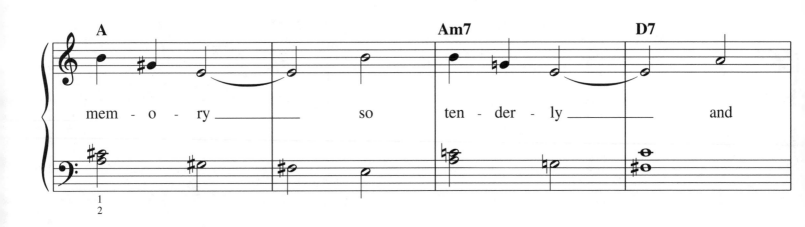

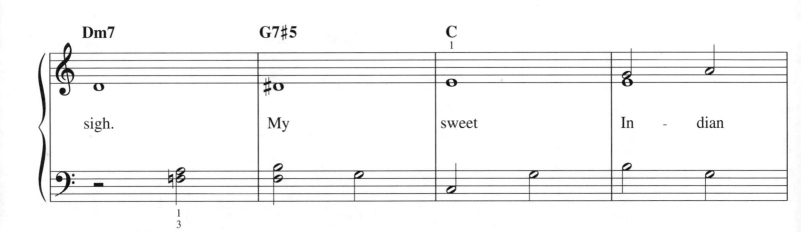

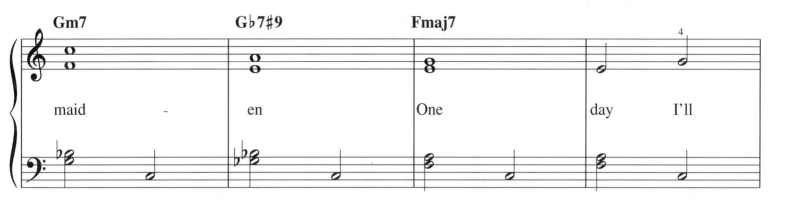

Gm7 ... G♭7♯9 ... Fmaj7

maid - en   One   day   I'll

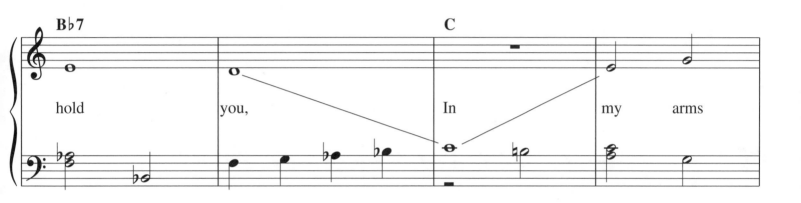

B♭7 ... C

hold   you,   In   my   arms

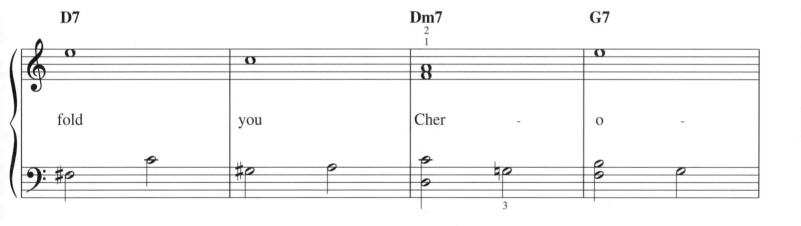

D7 ... Dm7 ... G7

fold   you   Cher - o -

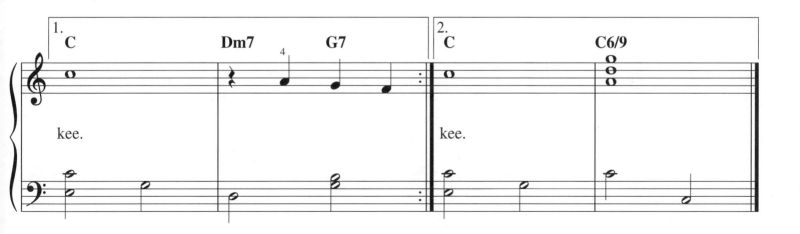

1. C ... Dm7 ... G7   2. C ... C6/9

kee.   kee.

DON'T GET AROUND MUCH ANYMORE

Words and Music by DUKE ELLINGTON
and BOB RUSSELL

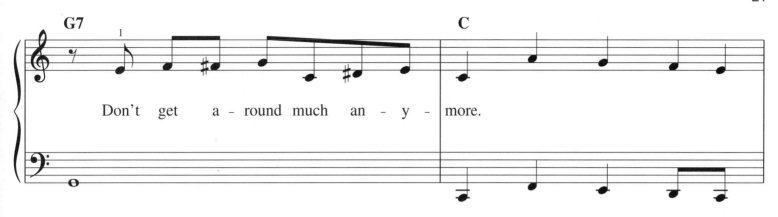

Don't get a - round much an - y - more.

Thought I'd vis - it the club   Got as far as the

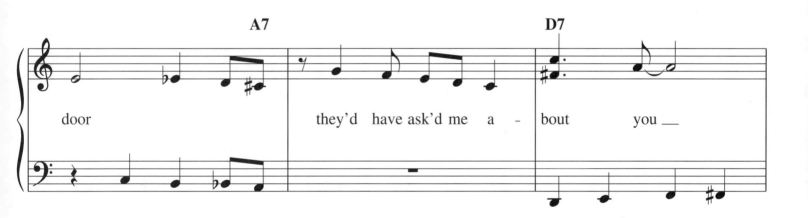

door   they'd have ask'd me a - bout   you __

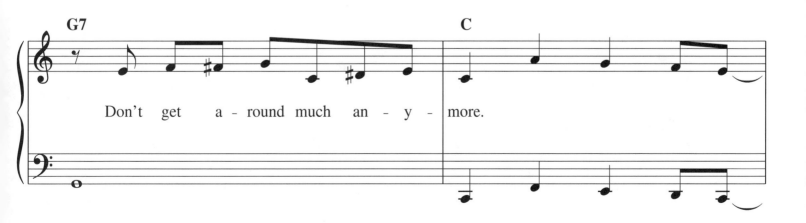

Don't get a - round much an - y - more.

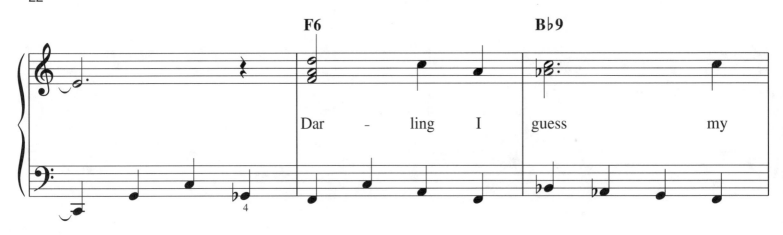

Dar – ling I guess my

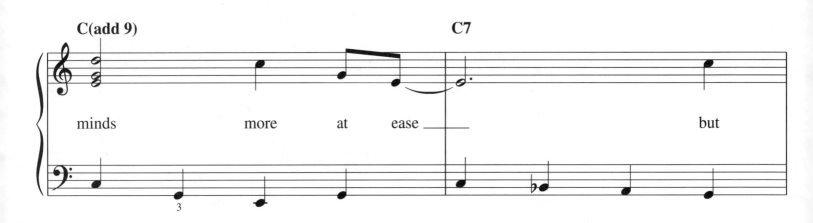

minds more at ease ____ but

nev – er – the – less why stir up mem – o – ries

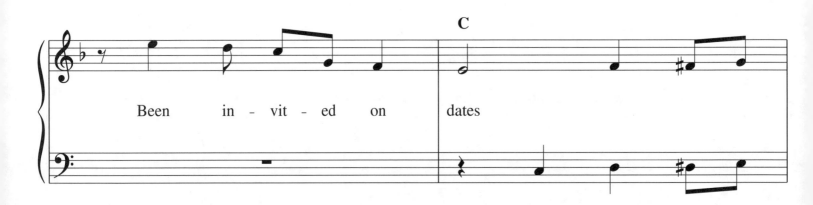

Been in – vit – ed on dates

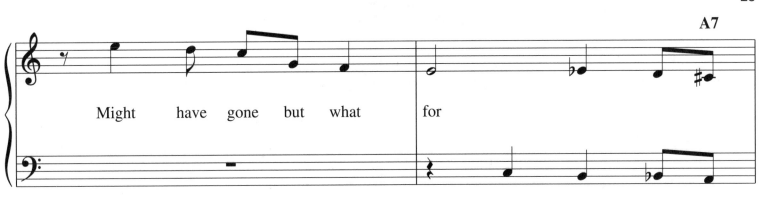

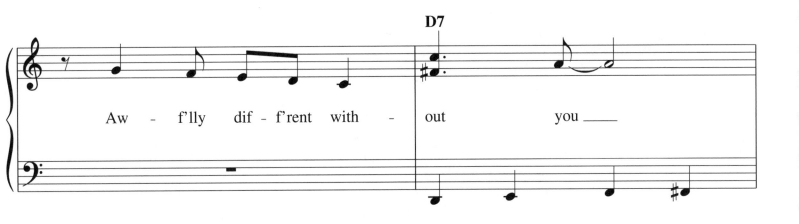

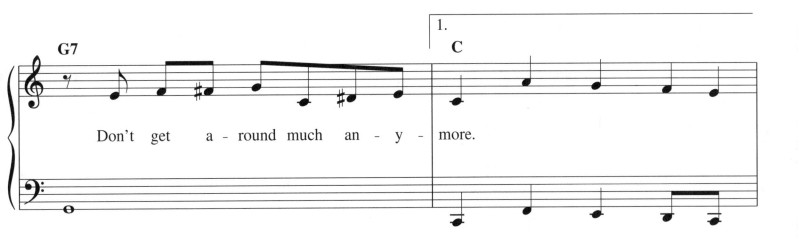

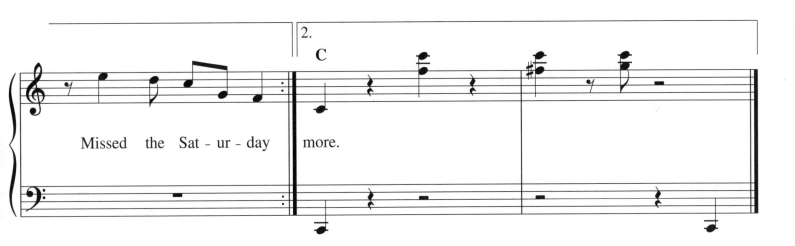

FRENESÍ

Words and Music by
ALBERTO DOMINGUEZ

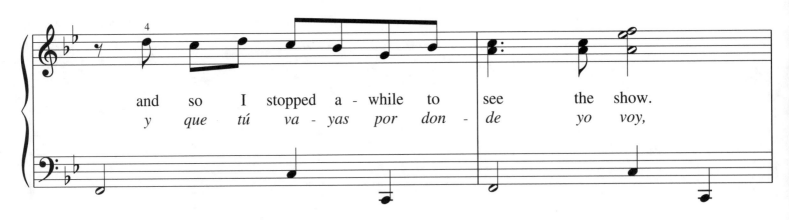

and so I stopped a - while to see the show.
y que tú va - yas por don - de yo voy,

Bb6   Bbmaj7

I knew that fre - ne - sí meant "please love me"
pa - ra que mi͜al ma sea no - más de ti,

F7   Bb6   N.C.

and I could say "Fre - ne - sí."   A love - ly se - ño - ri - ta
bé - sa - me con fre - ne - sí.   Da - me la luz que tie - ne

F7

caught my eye.   I stood en - chant - ed as she wan - der'd by,
tu mi - rar   y la͜an sie - dad que͜en - tre tus la - bios vi,

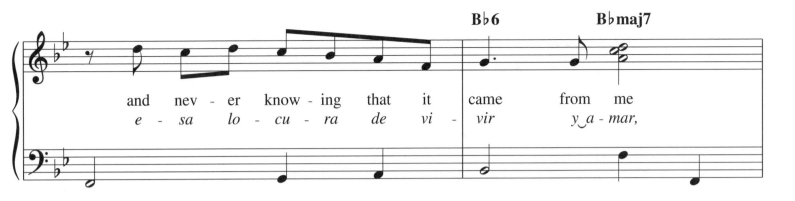

and nev - er know - ing that it came from me
e - sa lo - cu - ra de vi - vir y a - mar,

I gen - tly sighed "Fre - ne - sí."
que es más que a - mor, fre - ne - sí.

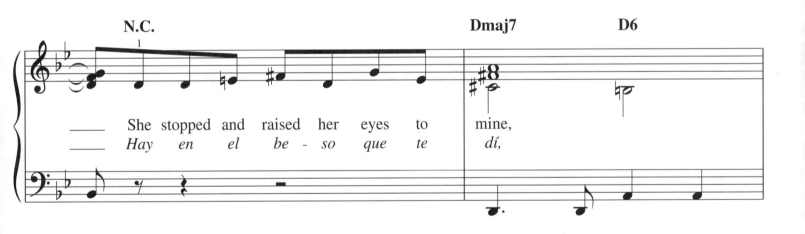

_____ She stopped and raised her eyes to mine,
_____ *Hay en el be - so que te dí,*

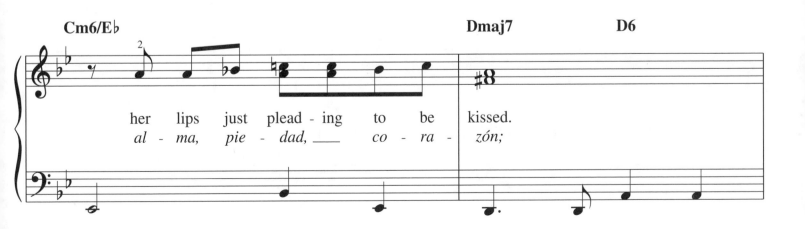

her lips just plead - ing to be kissed.
al - ma, pie - dad, ____ co - ra - zón;

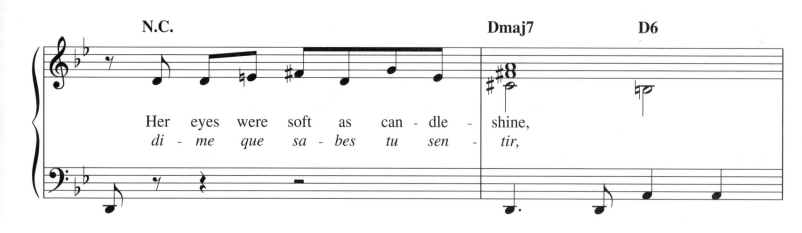

Her eyes were soft as can - dle - shine,
di - me que sa - bes tu sen - tir,

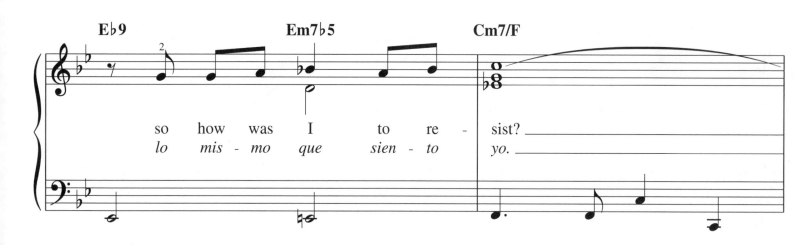

so how was I to re - sist? _____
lo mis - mo que sien - to yo. _____

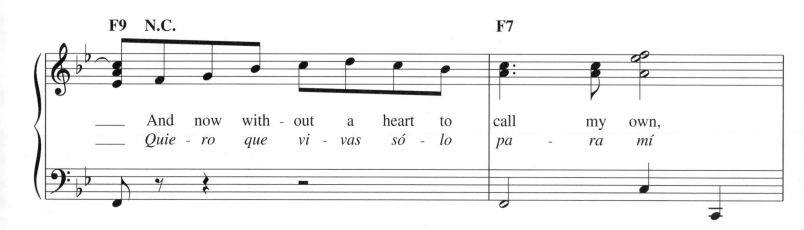

_____ And now with - out a heart to call my own,
_____ *Quie - ro que vi - vas só - lo pa - ra mí*

a great - er hap - pi - ness I've nev - er known
y que tú va - yas por don - de yo voy,

be - cause her kiss - es are for me a - lone,
pa - ra que mi al-ma sea no - más de tí,

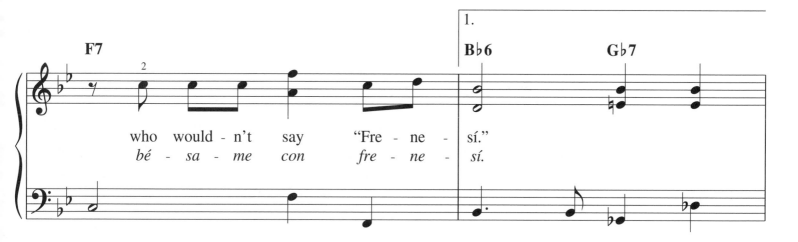

who would - n't say "Fre - ne - sí."
bé - sa - me con fre - ne - sí.

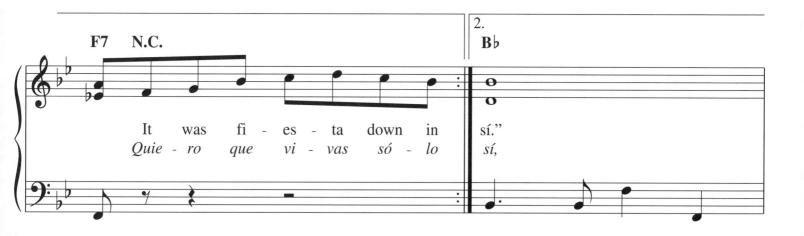

It was fi - es - ta down in sí."
Quie - ro que vi - vas só - lo sí,

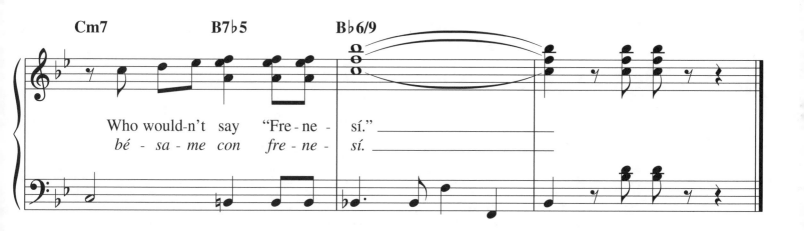

Who would-n't say "Fre - ne - sí." _____
bé - sa - me con fre - ne - sí. _____

I CAN'T GET STARTED WITH YOU
from ZIEGFELD FOLLIES

Words by IRA GERSHWIN
Music by VERNON DUKE

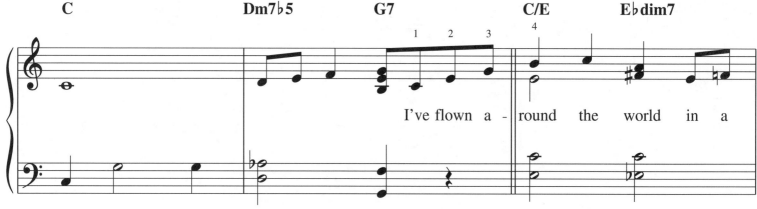

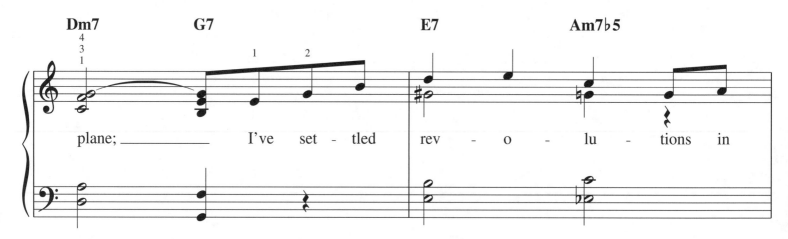

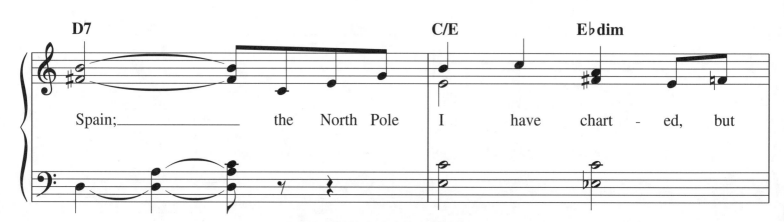

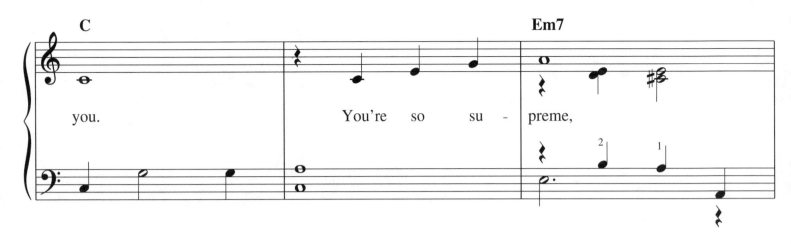

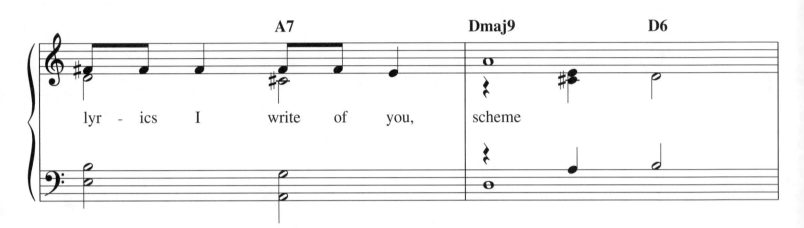

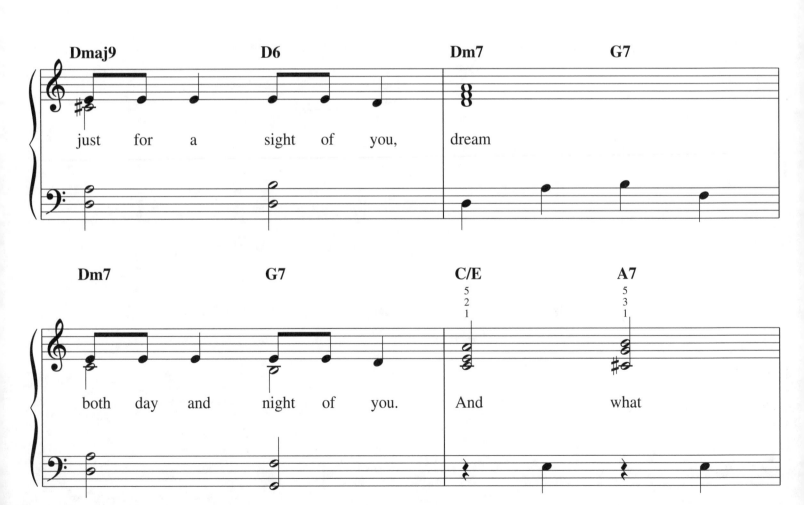

I'VE GOT MY LOVE
TO KEEP ME WARM

from the 20th Century Fox Motion Picture ON THE AVENUE

Words and Music by
IRVING BERLIN

Moderately

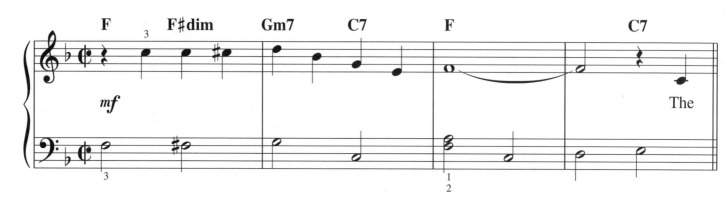

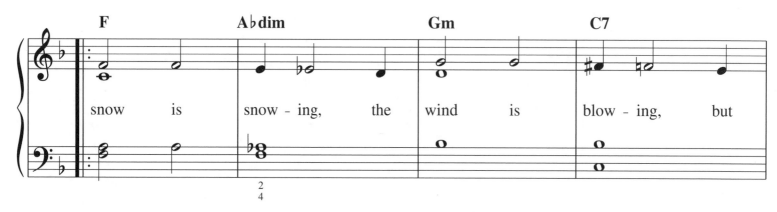

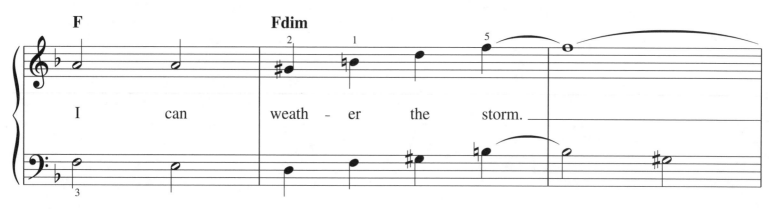

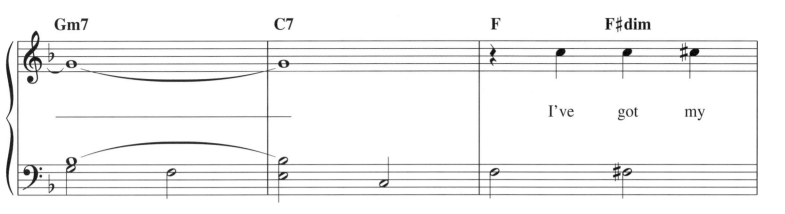

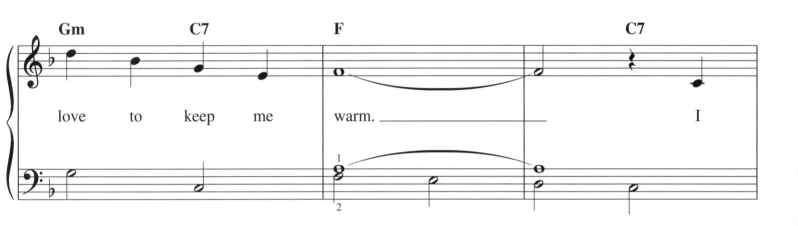

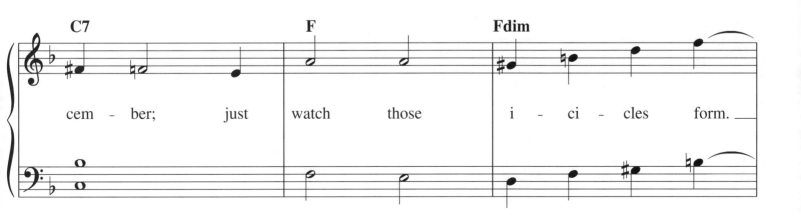

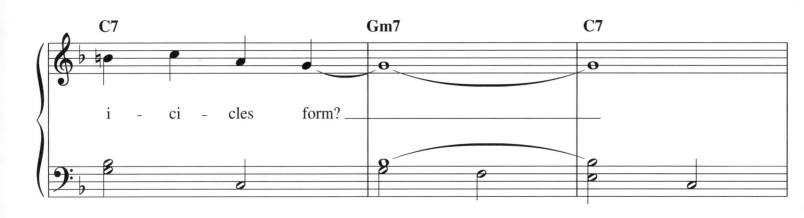

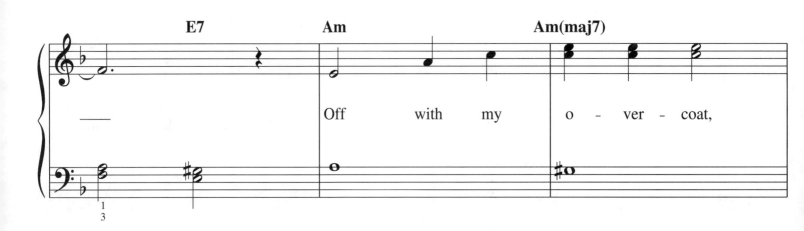

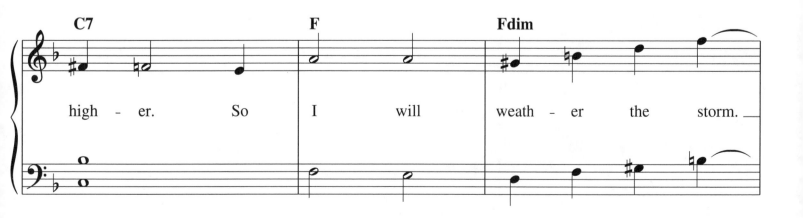

Gm7

What do I care how

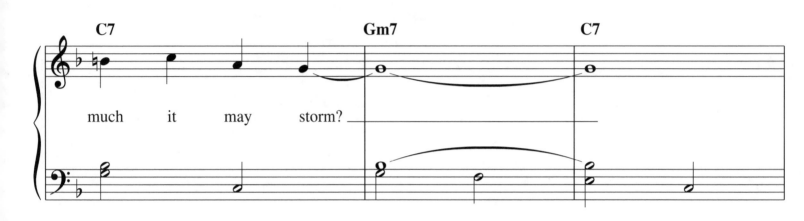

C7   **Gm7**   **C7**

much it may storm?

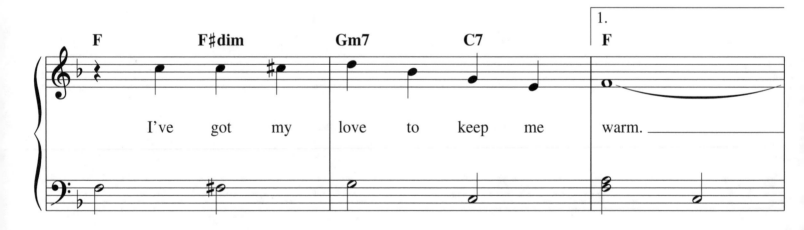

F   **F#dim**   **Gm7**   **C7**   **1.**   **F**

I've got my love to keep me warm.

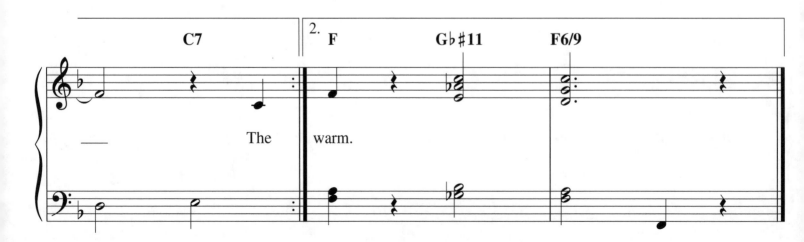

C7   **2.** **F**   **Gb#11**   **F6/9**

The warm.

IT DON'T MEAN A THING

(If It Ain't Got That Swing)
from SOPHISTICATED LADIES

Words and Music by DUKE ELLINGTON
and IRVING MILLS

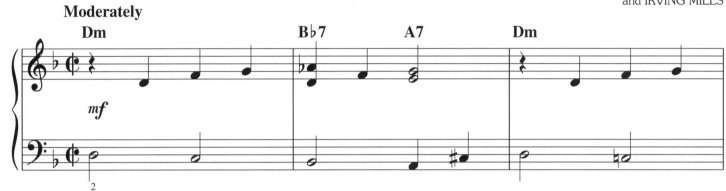

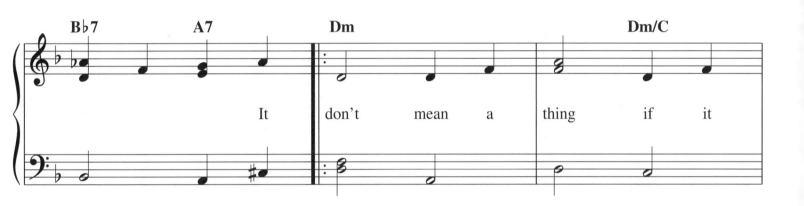

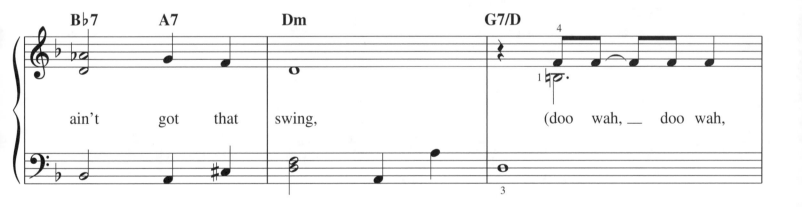

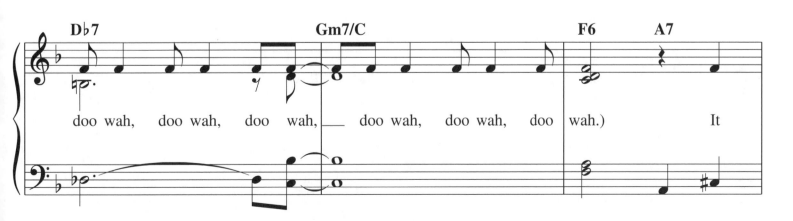

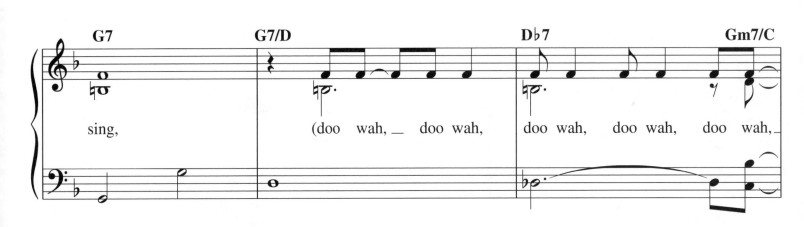

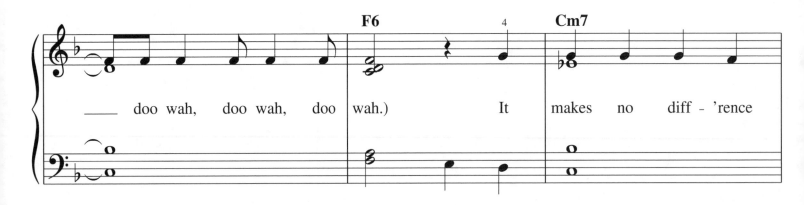

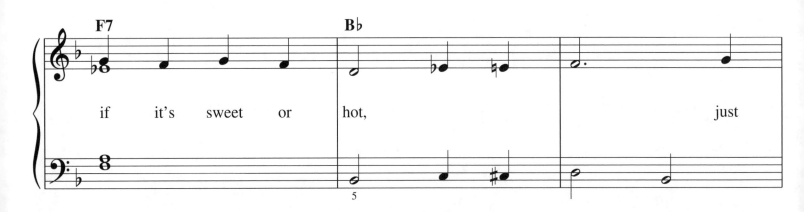

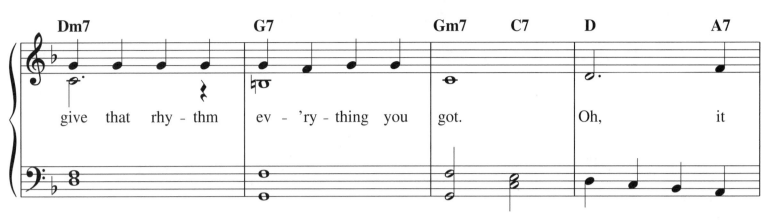

give that rhy - thm ev - 'ry - thing you got. Oh, it

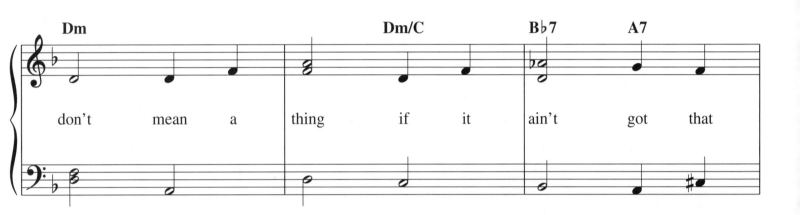

don't mean a thing if it ain't got that

swing, (doo wah, — doo wah, doo wah, doo wah, doo wah,

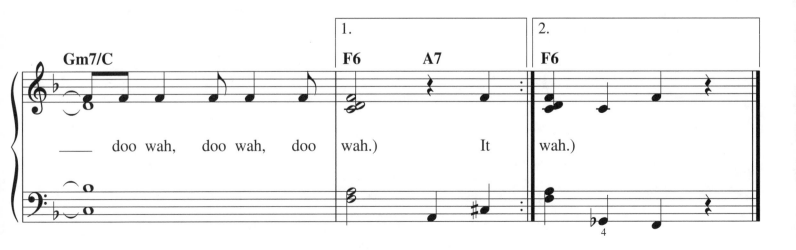

— doo wah, doo wah, doo wah.) It wah.)

IN THE MOOD

By JOE GARLAND

MOOD INDIGO

from SOPHISTICATED LADIES

Words and Music by DUKE ELLINGTON,
IRVING MILLS and ALBANY BIGARD

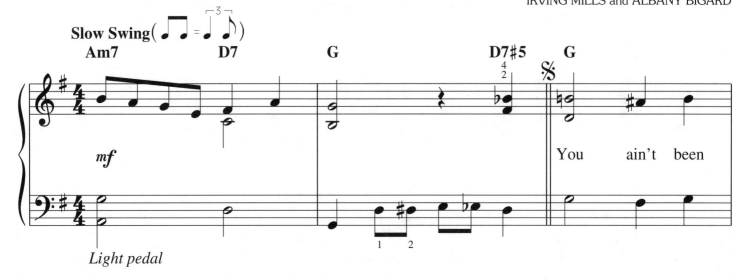

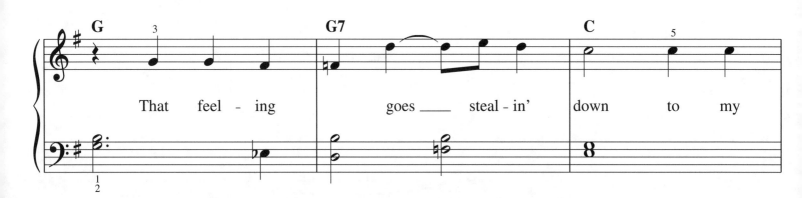

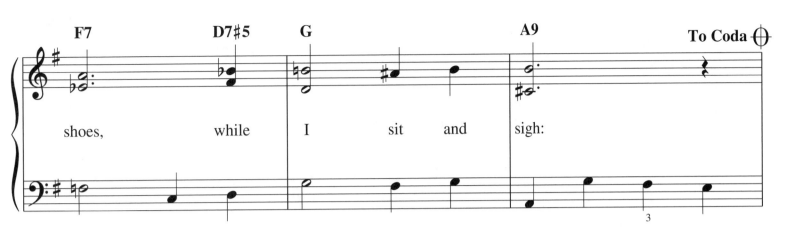

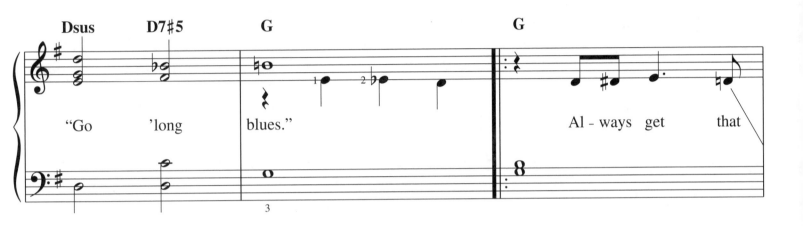

OPUS ONE

Words and Music by
SY OLIVER

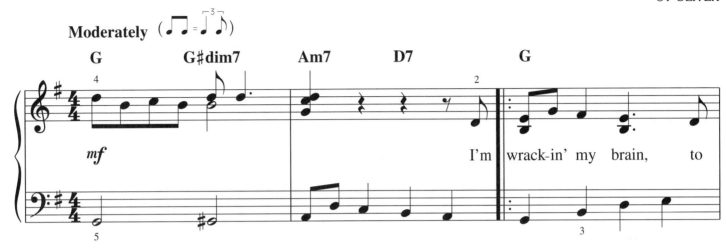

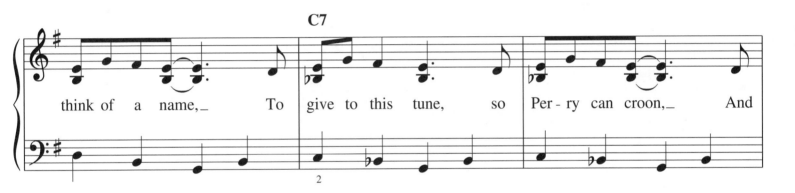

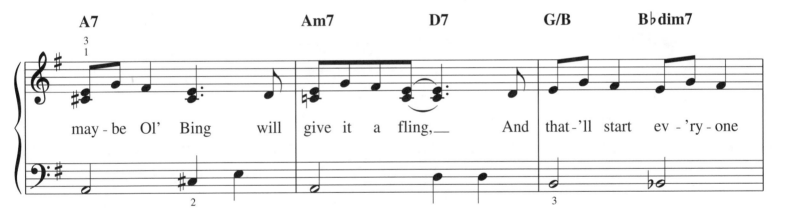

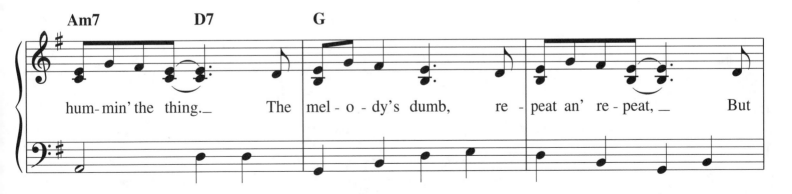

if you can swing, it's got a good beat,__ And that's the main thing, to

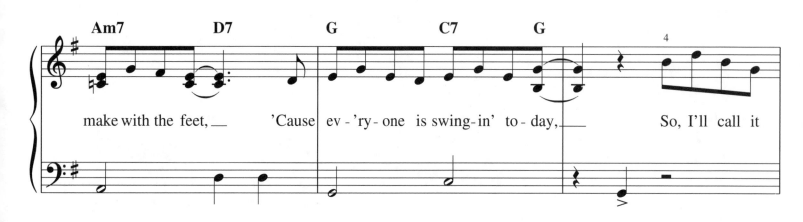

make with the feet,__ 'Cause ev-'ry-one is swing-in' to-day,__ So, I'll call it

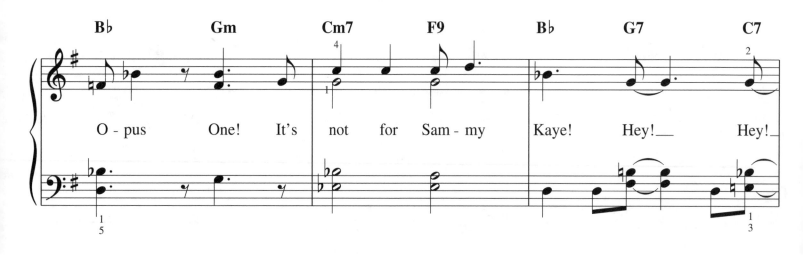

O - pus One! It's not for Sam - my Kaye! Hey!__ Hey!

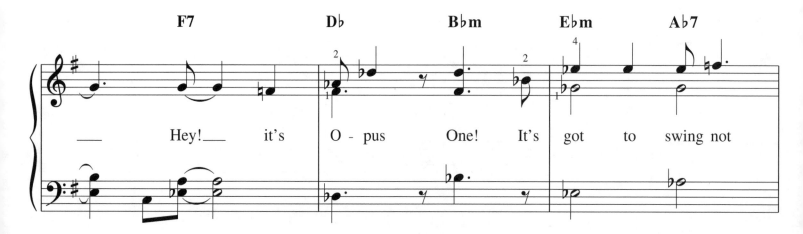

__ Hey!__ it's O - pus One! It's got to swing not

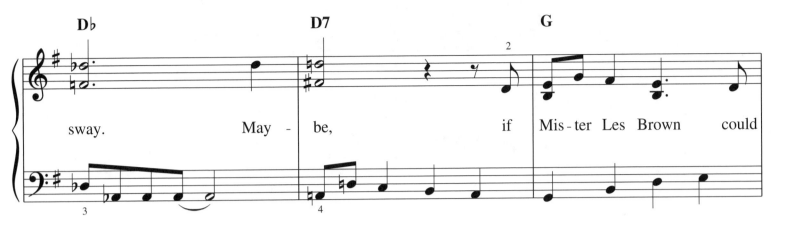

sway.   May - be,   if Mis - ter Les Brown could

make it re - nown__   And Ray An - tho - ny   could swing it for me,__   There's

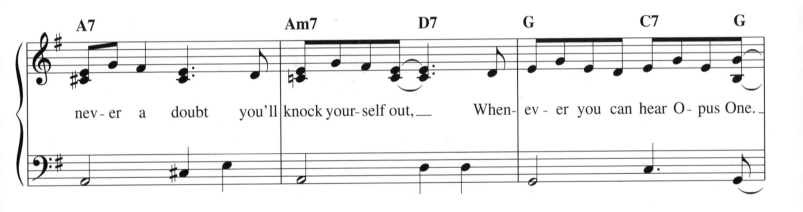

nev - er a doubt you'll knock your - self out,__   When - ev - er you can hear O - pus One.

1.   2.   Ab6/9 G6/9

I'm

A NIGHTINGALE SANG IN BERKELEY SQUARE

Lyric by ERIC MASCHWITZ
Music by MANNING SHERWIN

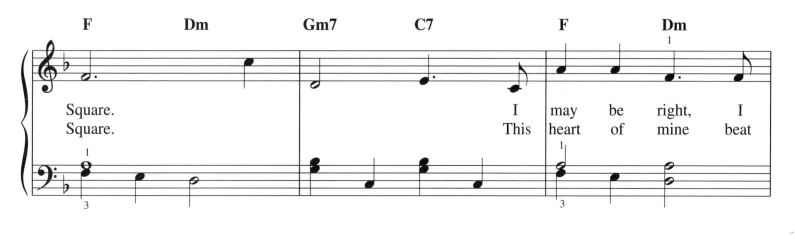

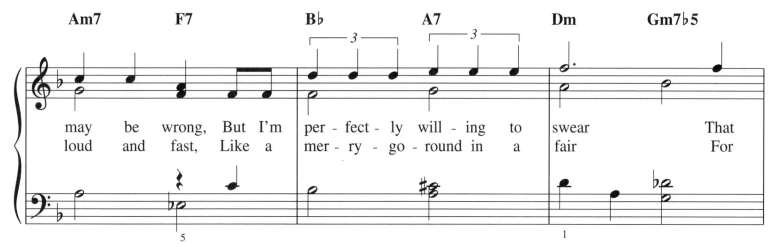

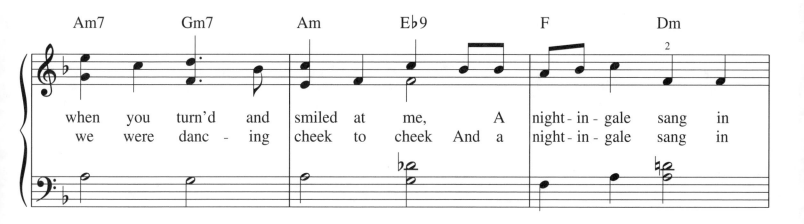

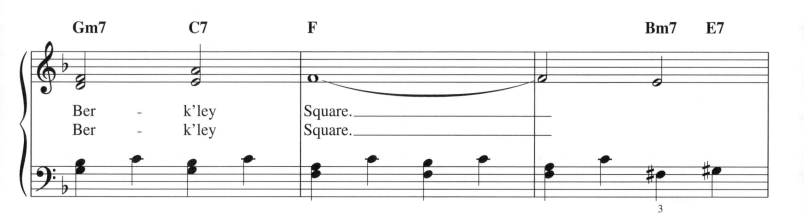

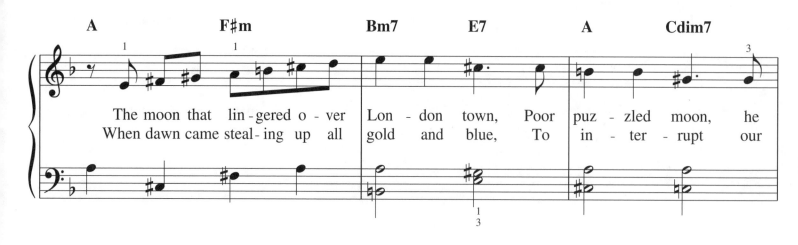

The moon that lin-gered o - ver Lon - don town, Poor puz - zled moon, he
When dawn came steal-ing up all gold and blue, To in - ter - rupt our

wore a frown, How could he know we two were so in love, the
re - dez - vous, I still re-mem-ber how you smiled and said, "Was

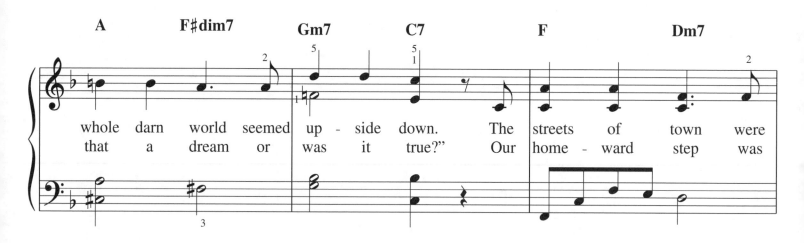

whole darn world seemed up - side down. The streets of town were
that a dream or was it true?" Our home - ward step was

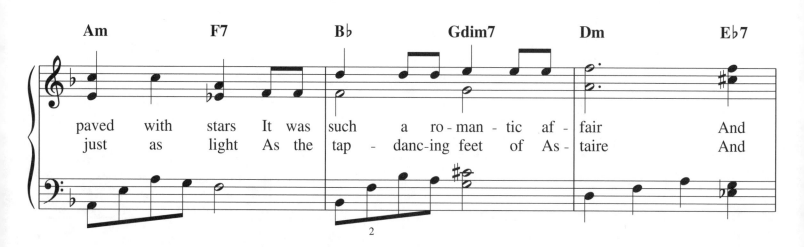

paved with stars It was such a ro-man - tic af - fair And
just as light As the tap - danc-ing feet of As - taire And

as we kissed and said "good-night" A night-in-gale sang in
like an e - cho far a - way A night-in-gale sang in

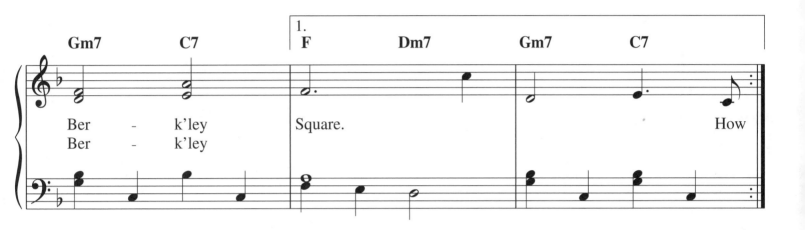

Ber - k'ley Square.   How
Ber - k'ley

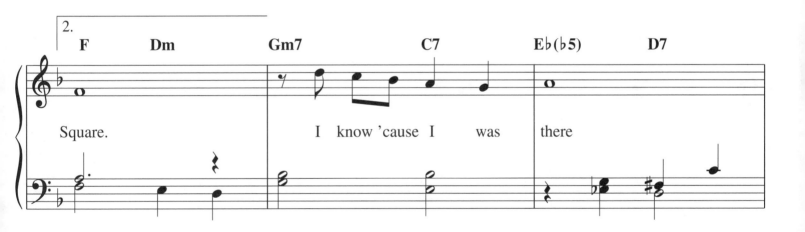

Square.   I know 'cause I was there

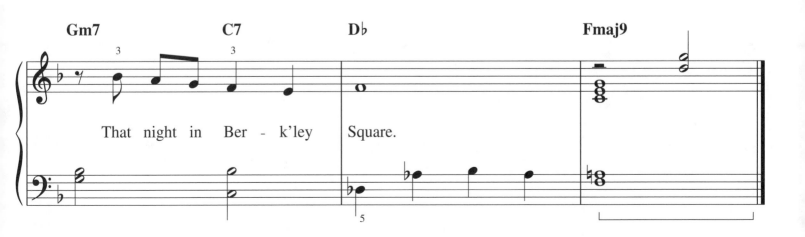

That night in Ber - k'ley Square.

PENTHOUSE SERENADE

Words and Music by WILL JASON
and VAL BURTON

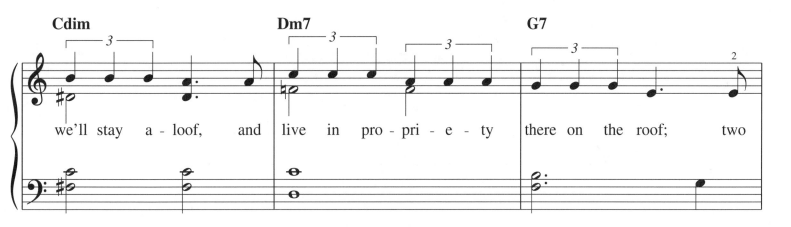

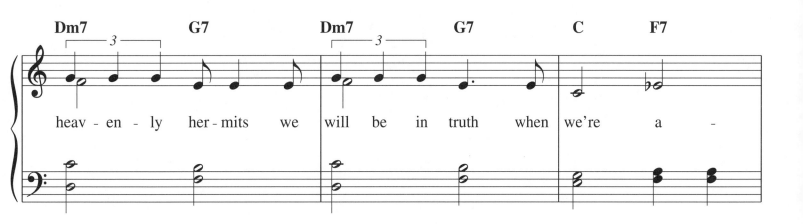

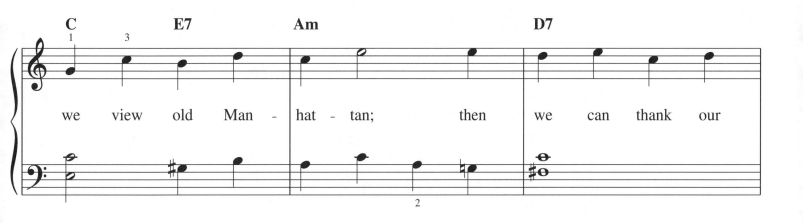

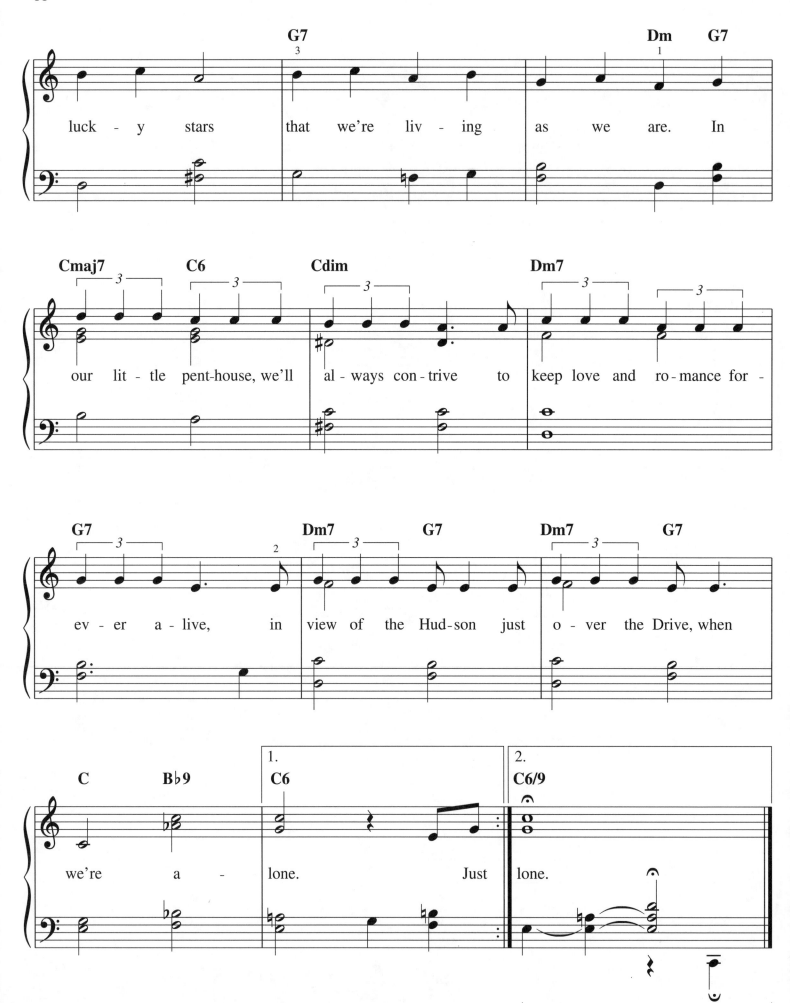

SOLITUDE

Words and Music by DUKE ELLINGTON,
EDDIE DE LANGE and IRVING MILLS

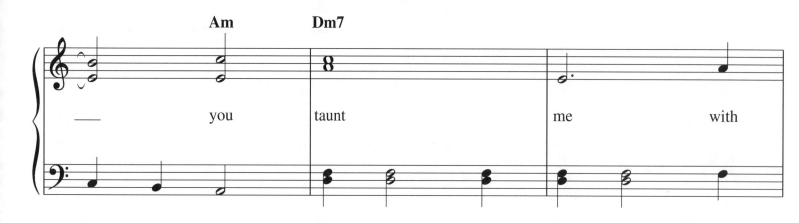

you taunt me with

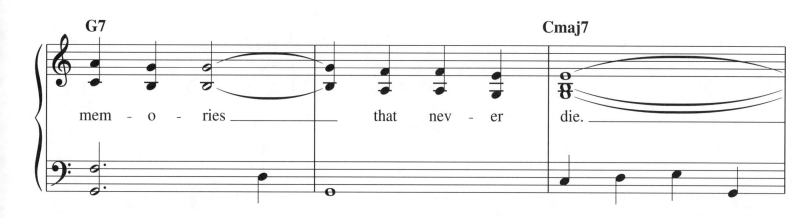

mem - o - ries _____ that nev - er die. _____

I sit in my chair, I'm filled with de - spair; there's

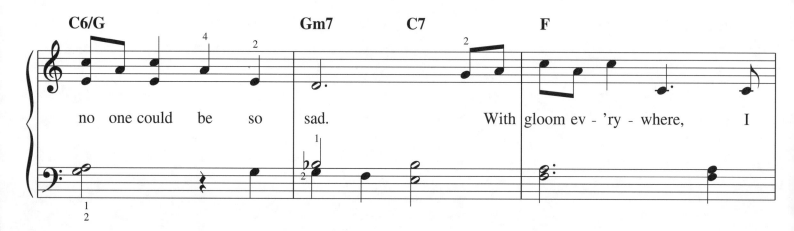

no one could be so sad. With gloom ev - 'ry - where, I

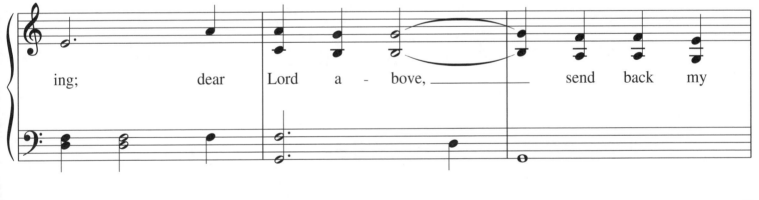

STOMPIN' AT THE SAVOY

Words and Music by BENNY GOODMAN, EDGAR SAMPSON,
CHICK WEBB and ANDY RAZAF

A STRING OF PEARLS

from THE GLENN MILLER STORY

Words by EDDIE DE LANGE
Music by JERRY GRAY

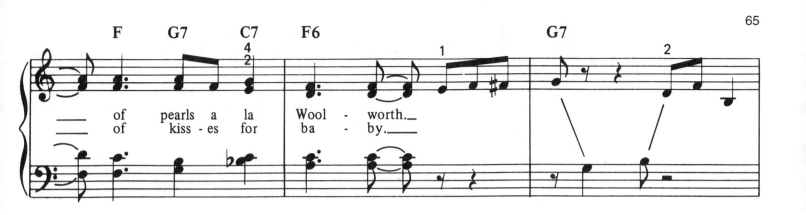

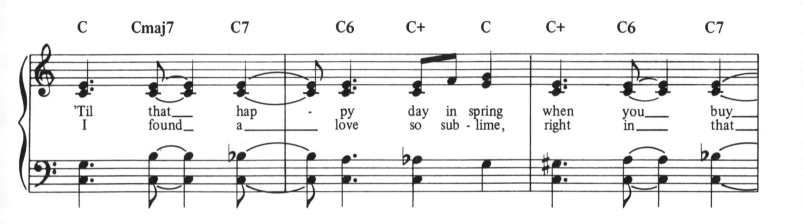

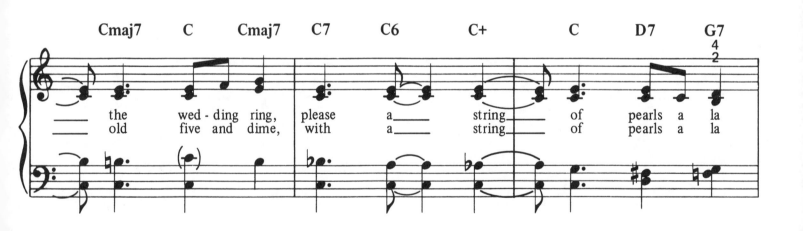

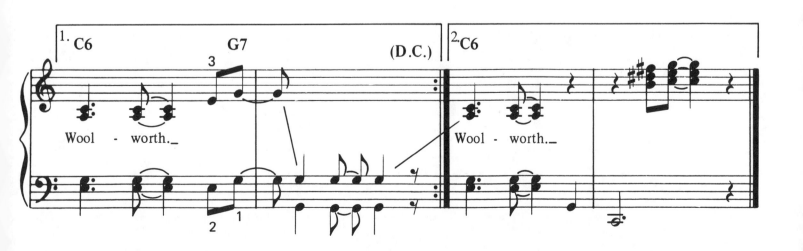

SUNRISE SERENADE

Lyric by JACK LAWRENCE
Music by FRANKIE CARLE

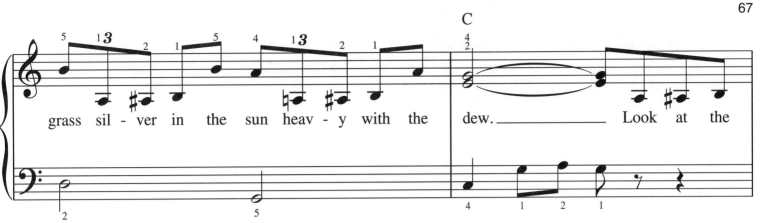

grass sil - ver in the sun heav - y with the dew._____ Look at the

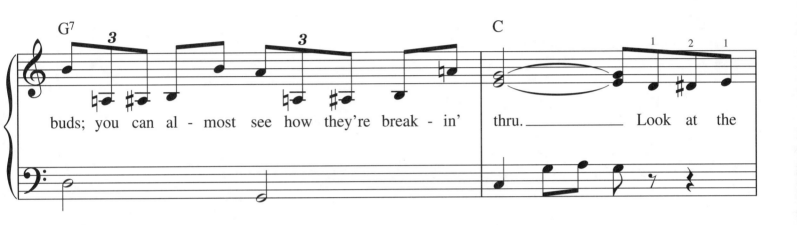

buds; you can al - most see how they're break - in' thru._____ Look at the

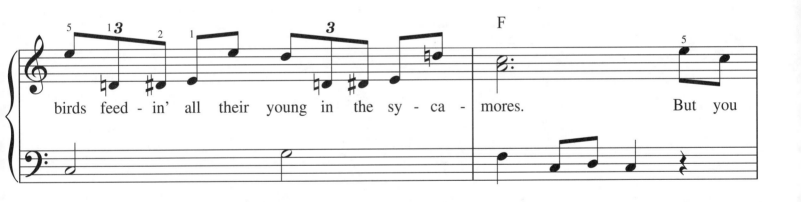

birds feed - in' all their young in the sy - ca - mores. But you

bet - ter get on with your morn - in' chores._____ Just take a

breath of that new mown hay and the sug - ar cane._____ Looks like to -

night there should be a moon down in lov - ers' lane. There you

go, day - dream - ing when it's time that you o - beyed that sun -

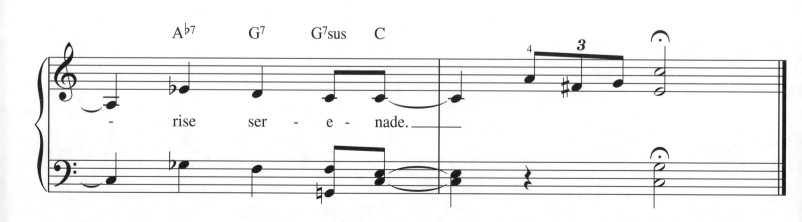

- rise ser - e - nade._____

TAKE THE "A" TRAIN

Words and Music by
BILLY STRAYHORN

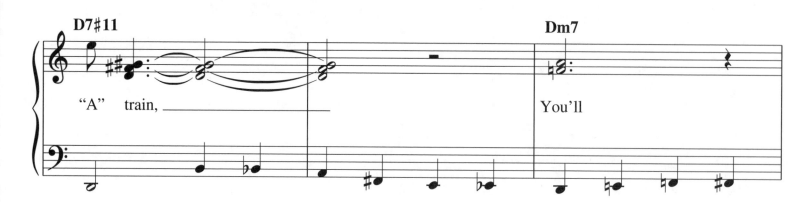

TANGERINE
from the Paramount Picture THE FLEET'S IN

Words by JOHNNY MERCER
Music by VICTOR SCHERTZINGER

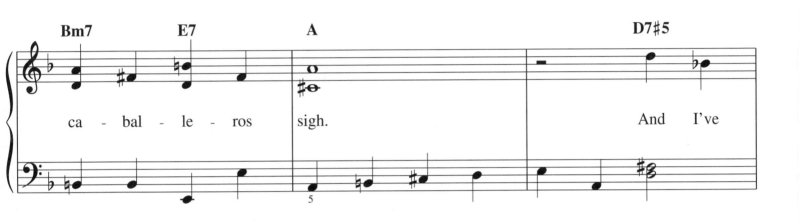

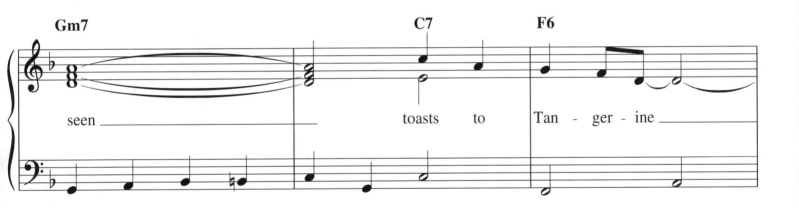

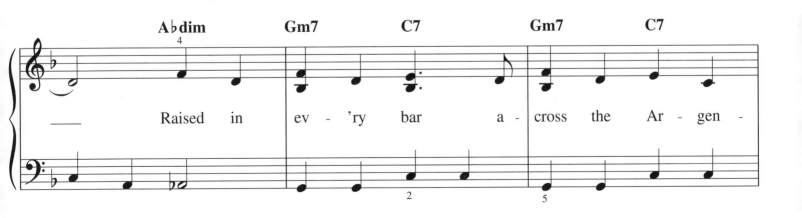

tine, _____ Yes, she has them all on the

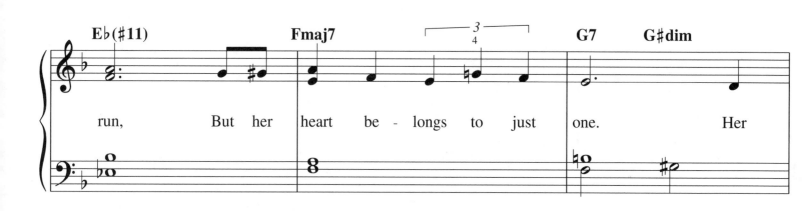

run, But her heart be - longs to just one. Her

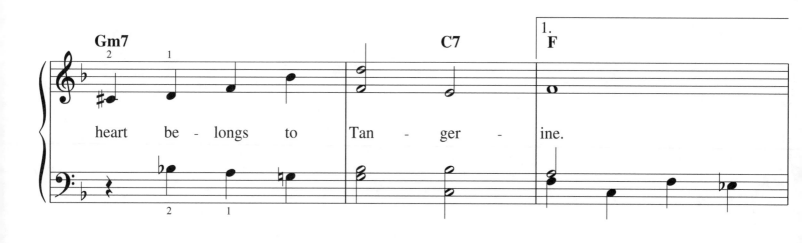

heart be - longs to Tan - ger - ine.

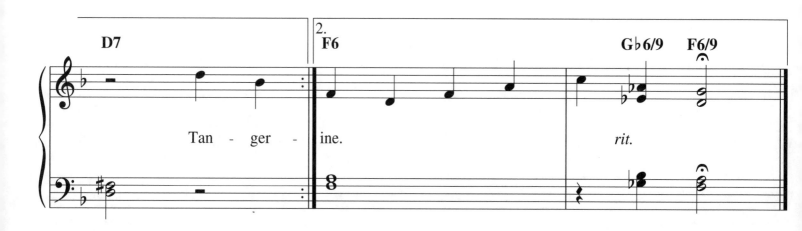

Tan - ger - ine.

THAT OLD BLACK MAGIC

from the Paramount Picture STAR SPANGLED RHYTHM

Words by JOHNNY MERCER
Music by HAROLD ARLEN

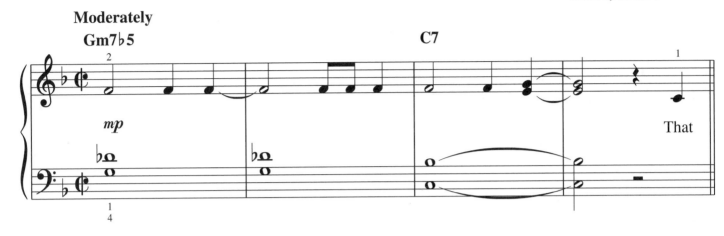

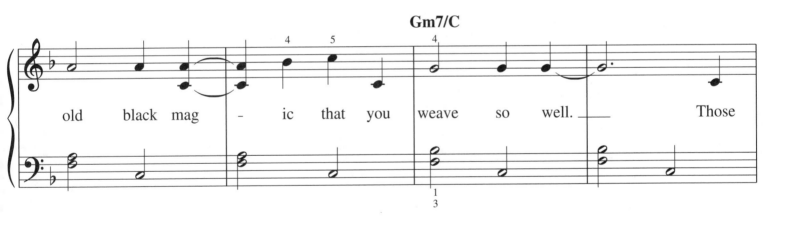

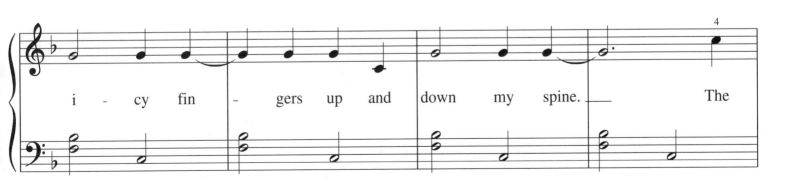

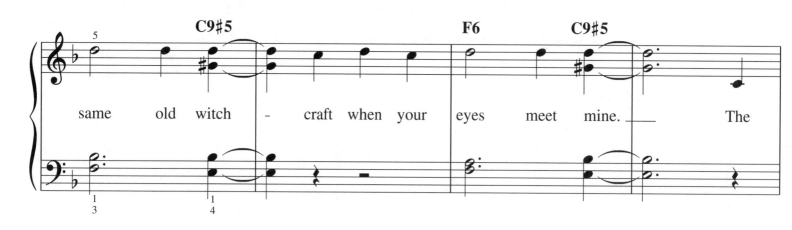

same old witch - craft when your eyes meet mine. The

same old tin - gle that I feel in - side, and

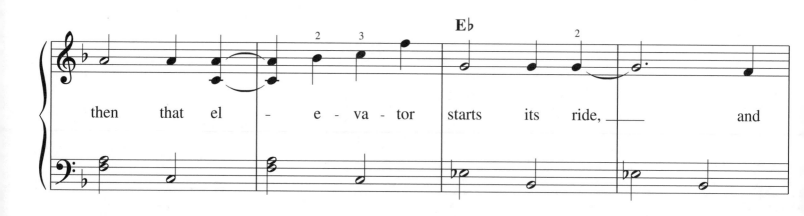

then that el - e - va - tor starts its ride, and

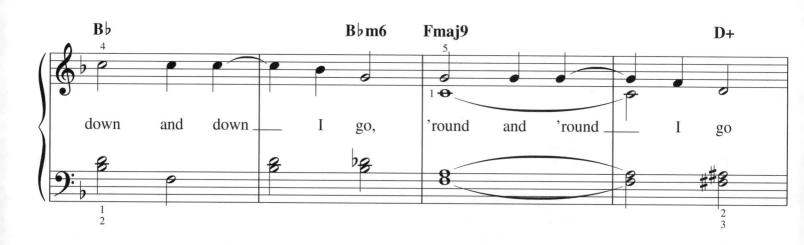

down and down I go, 'round and 'round I go

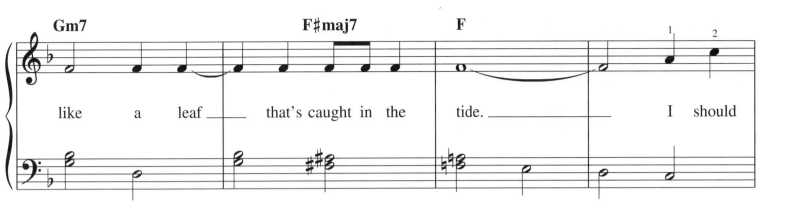

like a leaf _____ that's caught in the tide. _____ I should

stay a - way _____ but what can I do? _____

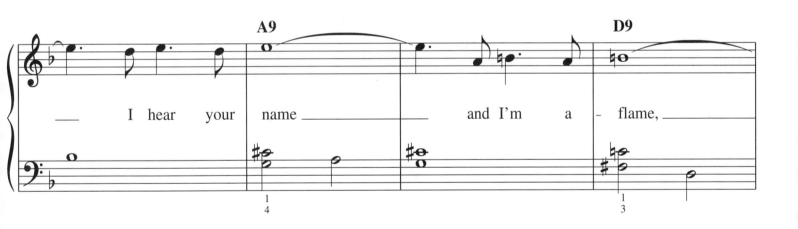

_____ I hear your name _____ and I'm a - flame, _____

_____ a - flame with such _____ a burn-ing de -

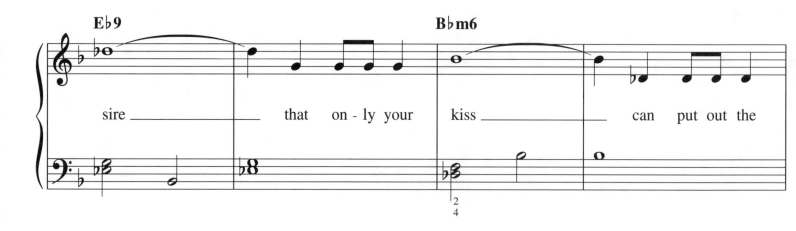

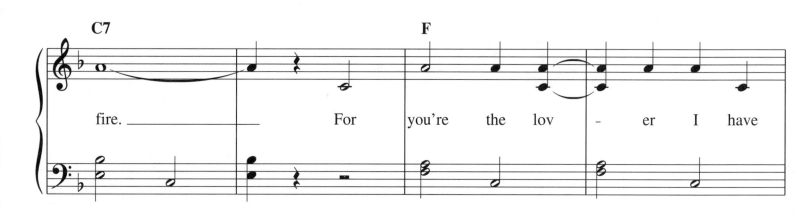

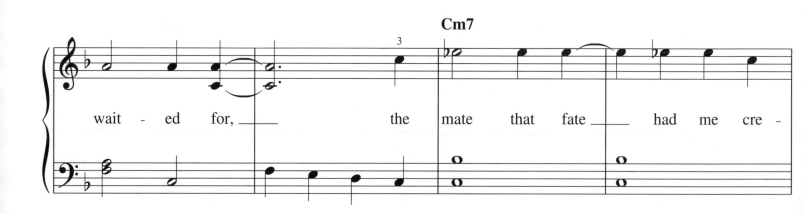

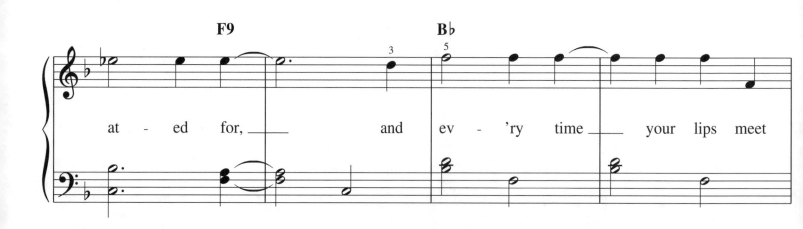

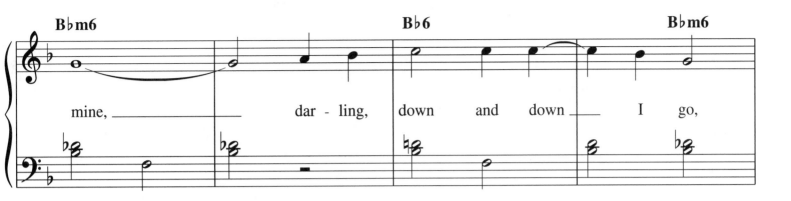

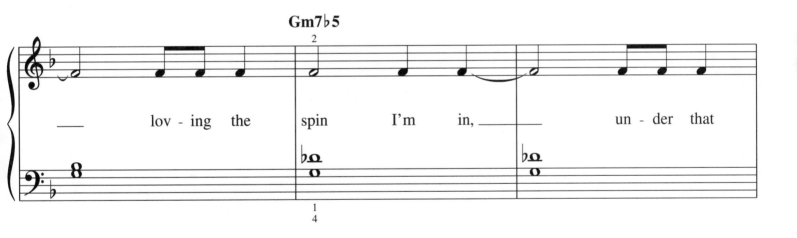

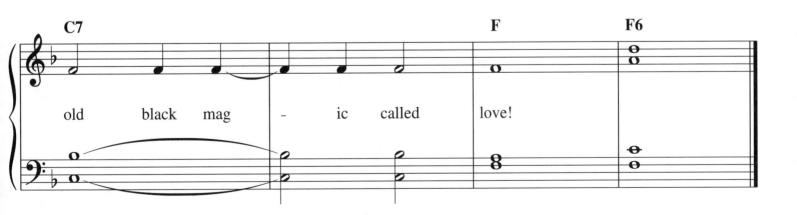

WHAT'S NEW?

Words by JOHNNY BURKE
Music by BOB HAGGART

Moderately slow

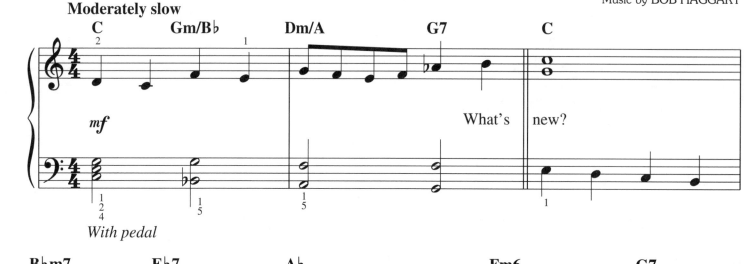

With pedal

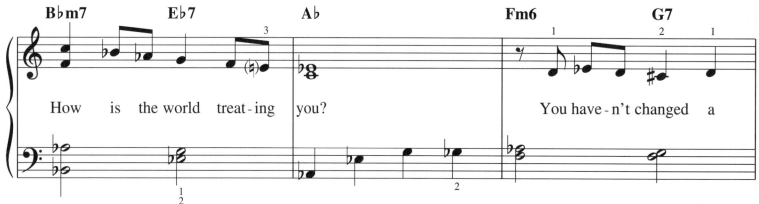

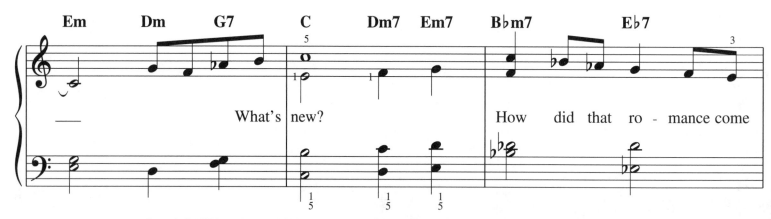

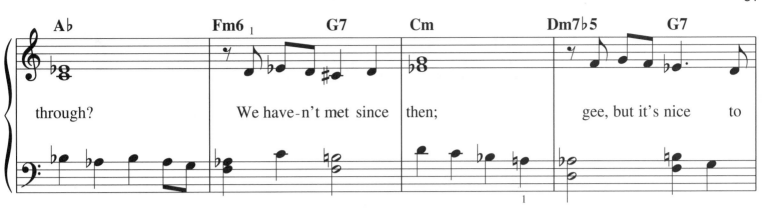

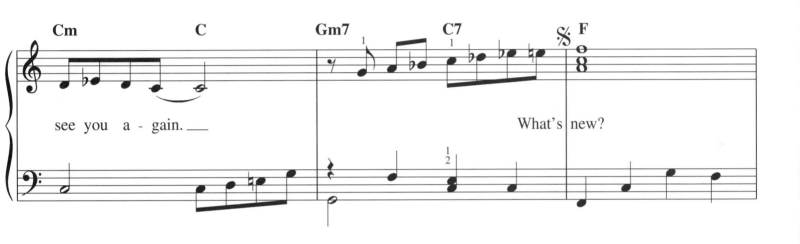

YOU BROUGHT A NEW KIND OF LOVE TO ME

from the Paramount Picture THE BIG POND

Words and Music by SAMMY FAIN,
IRVING KAHAL and PIERRE NORMAN

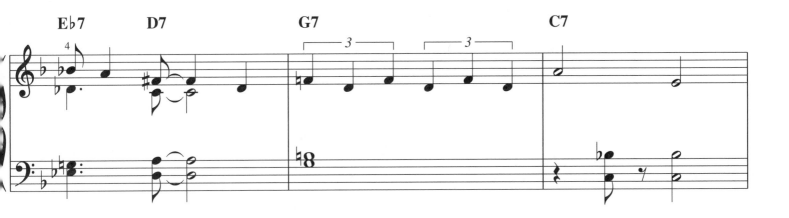

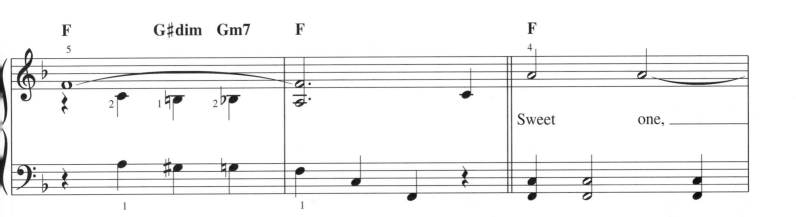

Sweet one, ___

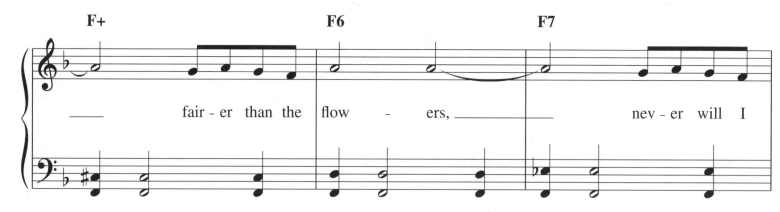

fair - er than the flow - ers, _____ nev - er will I

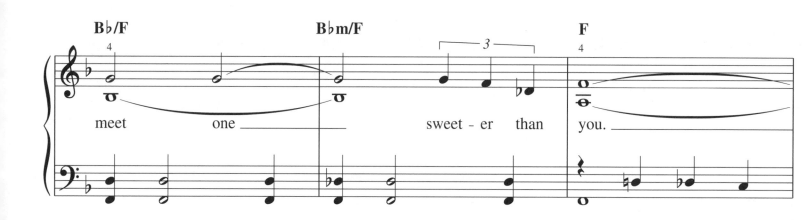

meet one _____ sweet - er than you. _____

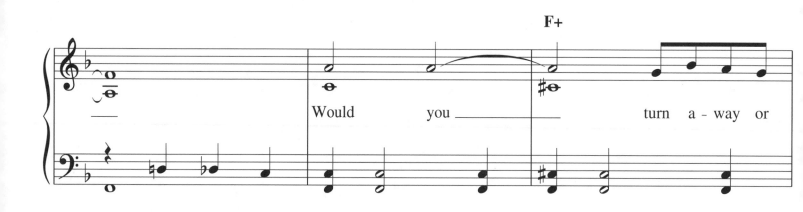

_____ Would you _____ turn a - way or

could you _____ real - ly learn to care if I'd ev - er

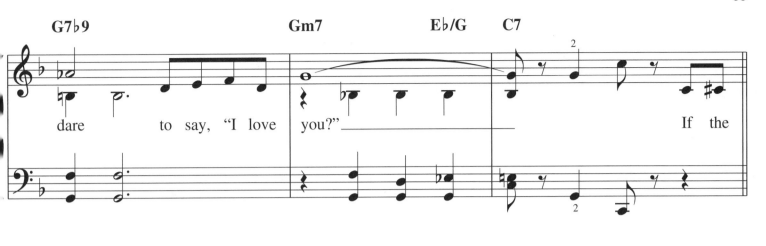

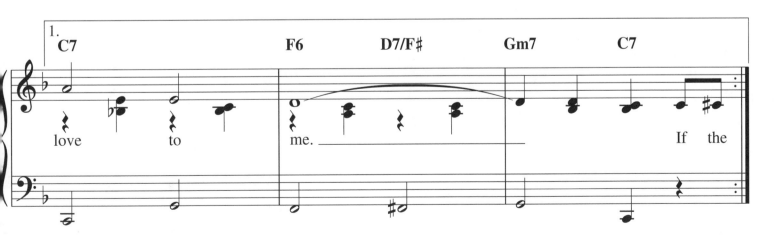

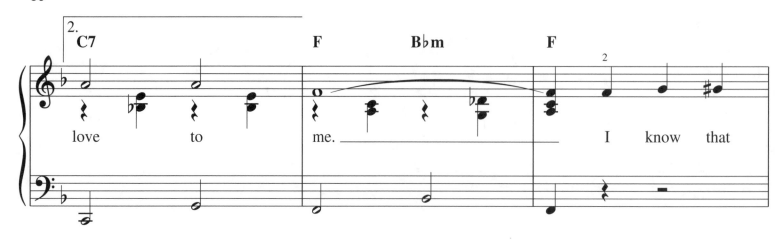

love to me. I know that

I'm the slave, you're the queen, but still you can un - der -

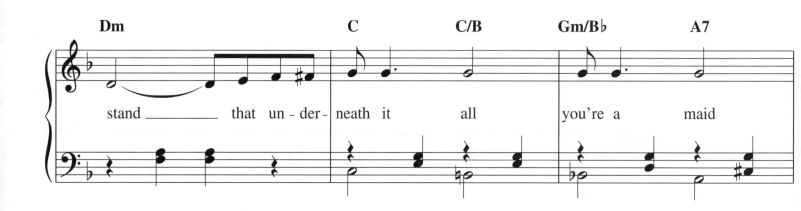

stand _____ that un-der-neath it all you're a maid

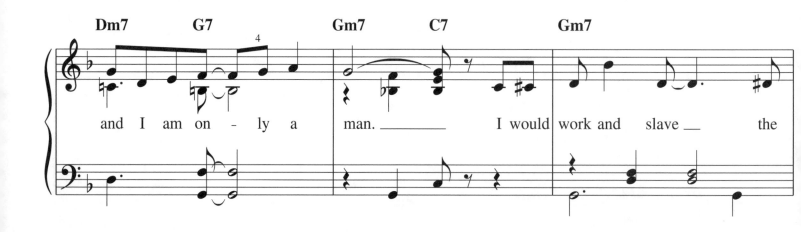

and I am on - ly a man. _____ I would work and slave ___ the

whole day thru, __ if I could hur - ry home to you, __ for

you've brought a new kind of love to me.

You've brought a new kind of love to

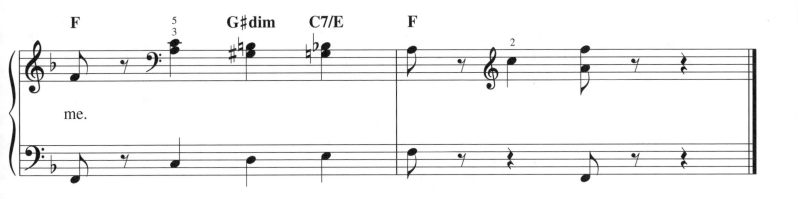

me.

It's Easy to Play Your Favorite Songs with Hal Leonard Easy Piano Books

The Best of Today's Movie Hits
16 contemporary film favorites: Change the World • Colors of the Wind • I Believe in You and Me • I Finally Found Someone • If I Had Words • Mission: Impossible Theme • When I Fall in Love • You Must Love Me • more.
00310248 ....$9.95

Rock N Roll for Easy Piano
40 rock favorites for the piano, including: All Shook Up • At the Hop • Chantilly Lace • Great Balls of Fire • Lady Madonna • The Shoop Shoop Song (It's in His Kiss) • The Twist • Wooly Bully • and more.
00222544...$12.95

Playing the Blues
Over 30 great blues tunes arranged for easy piano: Baby, Won't You Please Come Home • Chicago Blues • Fine and Mellow • Heartbreak Hotel • Pinetop's Blues • St. Louis Blues • The Thrill Is Gone • more.
00310102...$12.95

I'll Be Seeing You
50 Songs of World War II
A salute to the music and memories of WWII, including a chronology of events on the homefront, dozens of photos, and 50 radio favorites of the GIs and their families back home. Includes: Boogie Woogie Bugle Boy • Don't Sit Under the Apple Tree (With Anyone Else But Me) • I Don't Want to Walk Without You • Moonlight in Vermont • and more.
00310147...$18.95

The Best Songs Ever
Over 70 all-time favorite songs, featuring: All I Ask of You • Body and Soul • Call Me Irresponsible • Crazy • Edelweiss • Fly Me to the Moon • The Girl From Ipanema • Here's That Rainy Day • Imagine • Let It Be • Longer • Moon River • Moonlight in Vermont • People • Satin Doll • Save the Best for Last • Somewhere Out There • Stormy Weather • Strangers in the Night • Tears in Heaven • Unchained Melody • Unforgettable • The Way We Were • What a Wonderful World • When I Fall in Love • and more
00359223 ....$19.95

The Really Big Book of Children's Songs
63 kids' hits: Alley Cat Song • Any Dream Will Do • Circle of Life • The Grouch Song • Hakuna Matata • I Won't Grow Up • Kum-Ba-Yah • Monster Mash • My Favorite Things • Sesame Street Theme • Winnie the Pooh • You've Got a Friend in Me • and more.
00310372...$15.95

Country Love Songs
34 classic and contemporary country favorites, including: The Dance • A Few Good Things Remain • Forever and Ever Amen • I Never Knew Love • Love Can Build a Bridge • Love Without End, Amen • She Believes in Me • She Is His Only Need • Where've You Been • and more.
00110030 ....$12.95

Broadway Jazz Standards
34 super songs from the stage: All the Things You Are • Bewitched • Come Rain or Come Shine • I Could Write a Book • Just in Time • The Lady Is a Tramp • Mood Indigo • My Funny Valentine • Old Devil Moon • Satin Doll • Small World • and more.
00310428...$11.95

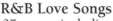

R&B Love Songs
27 songs, including: Ain't Nothing Like the Real Thing • Easy • Exhale (Shoop Shoop) • The First Time Ever I Saw Your Face • Here and Now • I'm Your Baby Tonight • My Girl • Never Can Say Goodbye • Ooo Baby Baby • Save the Best for Last • Someday • Still • and more.
00310181 ....$12.95

Best of Cole Porter
Over 30 songs, including: Be a Clown • Begin the Beguine • Easy to Love • From This Moment On • In the Still of the Night • Night and Day • So in Love • Too Darn Hot • You Do Something to Me • You'd Be So Nice to Come Home To • and more
00311576...$14.95

FOR MORE INFORMATION, SEE YOUR LOCAL MUSIC DEALER, OR WRITE TO:

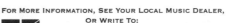
HAL•LEONARD®
CORPORATION

7777 W. BLUEMOUND RD. P.O. BOX 13819 MILWAUKEE, WI 53213

www.halleonard.com
Prices, book contents, and availability subject to change without notice